AF531178

Ke Ola Mamo
Native Hawaiian Health Care System, O'ahu

April 13, 1993

'Ano 'ai me ke aloha pumehana kakou,

On behalf of Ke Ola Mamo, the Native Hawaiian Health Care System on the island of O'ahu, I wish to extend a special mahalo to the Kawananakoa Family for their generous corporate donation of 300 copies of Linda Ching's recent publication, **'ANO LANI - The Monarchy Years of Hawaii Kingdom**.

Ke Ola Mamo, the Native Hawaiian Health Care System on Oahu is a private non-profit community based corporation whose mission is to improve the health status of native Hawaiians through a health care delivery system focussing on: health education, disease prevention, nutrition programs and accessibility to both traditional and non-traditional healing practices.

Your kind gift will further the goals and objectives of this corporation as it meets its mission of empowering our kanaka maoli pua to live longer and productive lives. Mahalo te Atua.

Mahalo a nui loa,

Agnes K. Cope, President
Ke Ola Mamo

of Heavenly or Royal Descent

With special appreciation to the sponsors who made this book possible:

Royal Hawaiian Shopping Center, Inc.

D. Māhealani / McCorriston-Martin
Land and Construction Company, Inc.

Hawaiian Electric Company

Edward Kawānanakoa

Hawai'i National Bank ◆ Sea Land Service, Inc.

Continental Airlines ◆ Otaka Hotels

Island Legacy, Ltd.

Library of Congress Catalog Card Number 93-070157
ISBN 0-9619891-30
First printing September 1993

Linda Ching, Publisher
754 Ilaniwai Street Honolulu, Hawaaii 96813

Printed at Toppan Printing, Hong Kong

Created in the Centennial Year of the Overthrow

of the Hawaiian Monarchy 1993

In memory of Zaneta Hoʻoulu Richards, a teacher.

You sought and searched for wisdom and truth.

"Nāu i noiʻi noelo aku."

...and along the way you touched and inspired someone

more than you ever knew.

Aloha

Photography, design and
text for photo illustrations by
LINDA CHING

Chapters 1, 2 & 4 by
MALCOLM NĀEA CHUN

Chapter 3
PAT PITZER

Layout & Typography by
KENNEDY DESIGN

Á NO LANI

of Heavenly or Royal Descent

ACKNOWLEDGMENTS

Anyone who has done a book knows that "book-birth" is like childbirth with its pains and joys. In doing this book, I've gone through a "pregnancy" full of frustration and doubt. For no particular reason, even when all is going smoothly, I tend to go through the same anxieties of an expectant parent who, at the worst moments, has considered adoption (to another publisher) and even has wondered out loud if the "child" would be okay. However, having gone through it once before, the second time around has its advantages. You know that there is a natural order of things with its own time and tempo. In the process, we learn once again that what is conceived with love most often results in a journey of miracles and fulfillment.

This "book-baby" has a wide extended family, some old and some new, whose nurturing input left an indelible imprint on the outcome. The generous support of many contributing in the true spirit of giving was part of the miracle of this project and a great part of the fulfillment. Much thanks goes to all contributors and my family of friends who held my hand through the gestation. From the pain comes great joy.

'Ano Lani would not have been possible without the support of my sponsors. A heartfelt thanks to them and all Hawai'i businesses, too often the unsung heros, who continue to be the supporting backbone of arts and education in the community. I would like to thank the museums and private collectors for allowing me to share their collections with you. ◆ To Don Medcalf for his expertise, remarkable collection of artifacts, for keeping me on track, and saving me from making some silly mistakes. To Roy Blackshear, David Cornwell, Don and Betty Lou Severson, Patrick Horimoto, Paul and Margaret Parker, Floyd Ho'opi'i, Donald Graham, Grandy Perry, Alu Like, Inc., Native Hawaiian Library Project, Bishop Museum, Hawai'i State Archives, Kamehameha Schools/Bernice Pauahi Bishop Estate Archives, Queen Emma Summer Palace; Daughters of Hawai'i, and The Hawaiian Historical Society whose collections fill these pages. ◆ Thank you to Malcolm Nāea Chun whose words brought vision and a unique dimension to the project. To Pat Pitzer for her words and wonderful editing. Mahalo Wayne Davis for the genealogy charts. To Naomi Carter for the beautiful lei she created for the dedication page. To stylist Leslie Galagher, Sheila Lau Davies, Arna Johnson, Louise Cavanagh, Stephen Ching, Margie Schnack Foytich, Manny Habon, and Lorry Kennedy for adding their own special touches. ◆ Deepest appreciation to the following for lending their support: The Hawaiian Civic Clubs, Ei-Rayna Adams, John Alves, Jo-Ann Arakaki, Michael and Linda Bottari, Gussie Bento, Puamana Crabbe, Barbara Dunn, Moana Eisele, Bruce Graham, Randy Iwase, Irving Jenkins, Ian Jones, Jalna Keala, Louis Kau, Bill Langer, Steve Gould, Holly Joy Lau, Creighton Liu, Warren Luke, Lydia Luden, Dilly Māhealani, William Martin, Bill McCready, Bill Morris, Phil Norris, Valery O'Brien, Michael and Joanne Parker, Hannah Pau, Gordon Pi'ianaia, Scott Shirai, Ted Sturdivant, Edward Stanley, Susan Sublet, Jack Sunderland, Carl Takamura, Lynell Totoki, David Uchiyama, Ron Wright, Elisa Udell, Leianna Woodside, Lani Yamasaki, Janet Zisk, and all the nice, helpful ladies at the Bishop Museum and Hawai'i State Archives.

Special thanks to Kaulana Kasparovitch for that gentle but firm push forward to do this book in the first place and last but not least, *mahalo*, Jose B. Lee.

Contents

Lizzie T. Newell

HAWAII

18 HAWAII 18
18 KENETA 18

INTRODUCTION

It is a belief of Hawaiians that their royal families were kin to the gods. The words *'ano lani* literally mean heavenly or royal in nature—heavenly or royal being one and the same. The gods and goddesses are defined by legends and myths in supernatural proportions, but Hawai'i's *ali'i* walked this earth within the bounds of human limitations. The monarchy years were marked with tumultuous expansion and change of lifestyle, religion, language, education, government and mode of dress. Old traditions, absorbed by the dominant western culture, went underground and were nearly forgotten. The hundredth year passing of the end of the Hawaiian Monarchy serves as a time to ponder . . . still close enough to touch, distant enough to gain some objectivity.

Heavy on the shoulders of the ali'i lay the future of a kingdom, and the perception of their people that they were guided by the divine. In search of who these people were and what they were like, I chose not to view them by deeds and data; rather, I tried to take a peek into their souls. Oftentimes it is easier to hold on to myths and legends than it is to search for the truth. I found the pages of history on the monarchy years thin, full of contradictions and inaccuracies. My curiosity led me to question what was behind the stoic portraits staring from within the archival folders. Who was the person beneath the personae? With this book, I offer my personal view of seven kings and a queen whom I tried to get to know through examining remembrances of those who knew them, by finding personal belongings that meant a lot to them, through reading personal letters, music and prose they composed, by investigating what the world they lived in was like and simply by asking a lot of questions. After months of research, I gained a lot of insight, and felt comfortably acquainted. Many of the artifacts I photographed are unavailable for public viewing either because they belong to private collectors or for security or preservation purposes. Some of my favorite archival portraits are previously unpublished. I've woven a collection of human interest stories with my own photographic tributes and tied them together with a text rich and full of insight written by Malcolm Nāea Chun, a contemporary Hawaiian scholar. It is with great pleasure that I share with you a short journey back in time and present another point of view of seven royal men and a lady to whom I'd like to say, "it was lovely to meet you, however briefly . . . I wish I could have lingered awhile longer."

Linda Ching

Á NO LANI

of Heavenly or Royal Descent

CHAPTER ONE

The glow of the second lamp lit that night flickered low as those who had come to eat with the ruling chief left. It was late at night, and in the closed confines of the thatched walls the crackling of burning *kukui* nuts mingled with the sound of men's voices. The only talking now would be among those who stayed

up with the ruling chief until the streaks of dawn stretched out across the horizon. Soon the third lamp, with its three strings of *kukui* nuts, would be lit as the circle of retainers, elder orators and chief counselors spoke of more serious matters and stories.

The flickers of light revealed the paler skin of the ruling chief as he lay on piles of plaited *lau hala* mats and finely beaten *kapa*. Rarely, if at all, did the ruling chief venture out into the sunlight. His realm was that of the gods, which was the night. He was born by their signs: the thundering sound of *pahu* [drums]

imitating the voice of the gods heard in the thunder and lightning. The tremors, mists, rain and rainbows marked both his presence and the gods'.

The ruling chief looked drowsy and sometimes nodded his head, having heard the stories too many times before. His indulgence to endure the night was for the younger chiefs, who had been gathered to hear the words of their elders. The young boys were wide awake and captivated as they listened to the orators reliving events that had occurred way before their own time. These men made words come to life as they told the story of a woman prophet named Wa'ahila. The ruling chief of the island of Hawai'i, Kalaunui'ōHua, hated her and swore to put her to death, but she was so powerful that no matter what he did, like cutting her to pieces at sea, beating her with clubs or throwing her over a cliff, it would not kill her. Finally, she told him that if he really wanted her dead, he had to kill her at a *heiau*, a temple, and have her body burned. Then he must be secluded in a house where he was to wait patiently for a whole day and night no matter what went on outside. If he did so, then her god, Kāne'openuioalaka'i, would ensure that the chief and his reign would have a long life.

Following Wa'ahila's instructions, Kalaunui'ōHua killed her and went into seclusion. When Wa'ahila's body was burned the smoke from the fire bellowed up into the heavens and formed the image of two chickens perched in the sky ready to fight. There was so much excitement at this sight that Kalaunui'ōHua wanted to come outside to see this phenomenon, but his people would not let him. The smoke then formed the image of a pig moving about the sky and again Kalaunui'ōHua wanted to see what was going on, but he was prevented from doing so.

Then the smoke turned into different colored clouds in a peal of bright flashes. The shape of two mudhens appeared in the sky and they seemed to fly down upon the gables of the house where Kalaunui'ōHua was hidden away. Unable to restrain himself anymore, he stuck his hand through the thatching of the house so he could see what was taking place. He did not realize that by burning Wa'ahila's body he had made her into a spirit. This spirit flew into and possessed his arm so that wherever he pointed it, a battle ensued in which his opponents would be vanquished.

Using his arm's magic power, Kalaunui'ōHua defeated the ruling chief of the island of Maui, Kamalu'ōhua. He spared Kamalu'ōhua's life and made him his *kia'āina*, the overseer of the land, for Maui. Kalaunui'ōHua then attacked the island of Moloka'i, and again by pointing his arm he won victory. The ruling chief, Kahoku'ōhua, was spared and was made the *kia'āina* of that island. Attacking the next island of O'ahu, Kalaunui'ōHua fought with Huaipouleilei, who was defeated and, like the other ruling chiefs, was made the *kia'āina* of his island.

At last attacking the island of Kaua'i, Kalaunui'ōHua endeavored to do the one task no other chief had done before, which was to rule over all the islands. That battle was called Kaweleweleiwi, the stripping of flesh from bones. Fighting Kaua'i's ruling chief, Kūkona, Kalaunui'ōHua brought with him his three defeated *kia'āina*. But before Kalaunui'ōHua could put forth his arm, the spirit left and possessed the arm of one of the Kaua'i people. Kalaunui'ōHua did not realize this and he pointed his arm, only to be defeated by Kūkona's forces.

Kūkona treated his captives with great respect and kindness. One day, he even stayed with them. Pretending to go to sleep, he listened to them. The captives believed that Kūkona was going to kill them, so they plotted to kill him first. But Kamalu'ōhua, the *kia'āina* of Maui, refused, saying that Kūkona had treated them well and though he had the opportunity, he had not killed them.

At that moment Kūkona got up and told them that he had heard their scheming, but because of Kamalu'ōhua's action they were to be spared, as Kūkona believed that life and peace were so important. The captives were sent back to their homes in "victory" to once again rule over their own islands. This was a time of lasting peace called *Kala'iloa* of Kamalu'ōhua.

At the ending of this story, the audience of young boys looked tired but entertained for that evening. The strings of burning *kukui* nuts were nearly extinguished, but the silhouettes of those lying about and sitting in the large room were faintly detectable, for it was nearing early morning.

The storytellers and the ruling chief wondered: Who among these young warriors would understand what this story was truly about?

The ruling chief could see some young faces looking disappointed. This story didn't end like the mock battles the boys engaged in each evening, where might and skill won or lost. These boys were quite good at throwing and dodging spears, fighting hand-to-hand and with clubs and slings. But it took more wisdom than knowledge to win and to rule, said the ruling chief to himself.

It was still dark outside and the air had a sharp chill. It was time to sleep. Another story, especially a long story, would take until the breaking of that darkness and the dawning of the light of the next day. There would be another night to continue his instruction to the young boy-warriors, he considered. One of them might just figure it all out and put it all together to realize his ancestors' dreams. The story of 'UmiaLīloa, 'Umi the son of Līloa, his own ancestor just a few generations ago, would be an excellent choice for a future night. It would match well with this night's long adventure.

With his neck cushion in place, the ruling chief relaxed into sleep thinking of how he could have been like 'Umi.

'Umi was a younger son of Līloa, the great high chief of the island of Hawai'i. An older son, Hākau, was born by Līloa's wife of marriage, and hence was the heir to his father's chiefdom.

Līloa had met 'Umi's mother when he had left the sacred ceremonies at Manini temple to take a bath. There at a stream he saw this beautiful woman and he fell in love with her. He asked her to sleep with him right then and there.

She told him her name was 'Akahikuleana and they were of the same line of chiefs. Līloa told her that if a son came from their union that day, the boy's name was to be 'Umi. He gave her his loincloth, his war club and his whale's tooth pendant—the sign of a high chief—to give to this son in acknowledgment that he was the boy's father.

Līloa went back to the temple wearing a makeshift loincloth of *kī* leaves. His people thought he must have lost his way and his mind. ʻAkahikuleana returned to her home and husband. She gave birth to a boy whom she named ʻUmi, but her husband thought it was his child. As ʻUmi matured, his foster-father constantly abused and beat the boy, until finally ʻUmi asked his mother if that man was really his father. She told him who his real father was, and ʻUmi said that he wanted to go to live with him. ʻAkahikuleana consented.

So the next time her husband was going to beat up the boy, she stopped him and told him that ʻUmi was not his son. He sarcastically replied, "Whose boy is he, Līloa's?" When she said the boy was indeed Līloa's, he demanded proof and ʻAkahikuleana got out Līloa's gifts and put them on ʻUmi.

Before the boy left, ʻAkahikuleana told him what he must do when he got to Waipiʻo to get around Līloa's guards and make his real father recognize him. He was to climb over the fence enclosure and slip into a side doorway, then quickly jump onto the old man's lap and proclaim that he was ʻUmi.

With these instructions, ʻUmi left with ʻAkahikuleana's brother, ʻŌmaʻokamau, who carried Līloa's club. Along the way they met another boy named Piʻimaiwaʻa whom ʻUmi befriended. When they got to Waipiʻo they saw Līloa's house and everything was laid out as ʻUmi's mother had said. He dodged the guards by climbing over the fence and sneaking through the side door. One of the head guards saw ʻUmi and rushed forward to kill him, but ʻUmi was quick enough to jump up onto Līloa's lap.

Līloa was so surprised that he opened up his legs and ʻUmi fell down to the ground. Then the old man saw that this boy was wearing his whale's tooth pendant and his *malo* (loincloth). "What is your name, boy?" asked the high chief. "I am ʻUmi, your son!" replied the boy on the ground. Līloa was so overjoyed. He picked up the boy and they touched noses as a sign of affection.

ʻUmi told his father everything that had happened. Then Līloa asked where his club was, so ʻUmi called ʻŌmaʻokamau and Piʻimaiwaʻa to come in.

Finally Līloa told all the people of his household that the day they thought he went crazy wearing the *kī* leaf loincloth he had actually given his loincloth, club and whale's tooth pendant away for his son, ʻUmi.

While all of this activity was going on, Hākau, the oldest son of Līloa, heard about this new younger brother and he was enraged with jealousy. So to appease his older son, Līloa told Hākau that he would be the superior over all, and would inherit his lands when he died, but Līloa's god and house would go to ʻUmi to take care of. However, Hākau's hatred for ʻUmi still grew, so when the old man died Hākau continued his abuse of ʻUmi. Fearing for his life, ʻUmi ran away.

With ʻŌmaʻokamau and Piʻimaiwaʻa, ʻUmi hid in the countryside away from Hākau. They settled with the people of the countryside and married women from there. But hiding ʻUmi was not easy, for as a high chief he did no hard labor, which upset his in-laws as they did not know that he was the son of Līloa.

One day a man of chiefly rank named KaleioKū, who had noticed many rainbows in the countryside and at sea where ʻUmi fished, figured out that there must be a high-ranking chief in their midst. He followed a rainbow, which led him to ʻUmi, then he released a pig that could search out a chief. The pig ran straight to 'Umi. They returned back to the country people where 'Umi's identity was revealed. Many people began to pledge their allegiance to 'Umi because he was able to feed and to take care of them. Unlike 'Umi, Hākau mistreated his own people, so two of his leading priests plotted to get rid of Hākau. They had heard about 'Umi and went to find him. KaleioKū arranged for them to be welcomed but he made sure before the priests arrived that they would only find 'Umi there. When they did arrive they found only one person but nonetheless, they were welcomed and fed. When it was revealed to the priests that they had been taken care of so lavishly by 'Umi, they were shocked and embarrassed. Never had a high chief humbled himself to serve others lower in rank and status. This impressed the two priests and they knew then and there that this was their chief.

The two revealed their plan to 'Umi. If he and his people would come to the new temple ceremonies bearing weapons and spears disguised as gifts and offerings, they would be able to catch Hākau off guard. When 'Umi and his legion arrived, they were noticed too late and Hākau and his followers were slaughtered by 'Umi's rebellion.

So 'Umi the son of Līloa defeated his older half-brother, who was despised by so many for his cruelty. 'Umi's god and the priests showed him favor and he was remembered as a chief who took care of his people in need.

But that is not the end of this famous story. 'Umi, with the help of his companions, was able to unite all the districts of the island of Hawai'i under one chiefdom. No one had done such a deed before. His reign was known for its peace and he continued to look after the welfare of his people, to establish laws to protect them and he continued to be a religious chief.

The early 19th-century Native Hawaiian scholar Davida Malo and the later 19th century Hawaiian historian Samuel Mānaiakalani Kamakau recorded that there was a young warrior chief who did listen and understand what those two stories had to say about how to unite the fiercely independent district chiefs and the ruling chiefs of the various islands. He understood what was required to rule with wisdom so that one's reign would last more than a lifetime, and last in peace. That young chief was Kamehameha. Malo wrote:

"There were many kinds of chiefs. They were not alike. Some plundered, others stole, or murdered while others collected [taxes and tribute] and others pillaged. There were very few who lived virtuously like Kamehameha I, who was a chief that ensured care and protection."

Kamehameha inherited the war god of the island of Hawai'i's ruling chief, Kalani'ōpu'u, while the land was given to the chief's son Kiwala'ō Kaukeaouli. Through his military skill, nurturing, and carefully made alliances, and respect for his priests and prophets, Kamehameha was able to duplicate 'Umi's uniting of the independent district chiefs of the island of Hawai'i. As if following the story of Kalaunui'ōhua, Kamehameha then proceeded to unite all the islands under one rule, his. Although, like Kalaunui'ōhua, he was not able to defeat the ruling chief of the island of Kaua'i, Kamehameha was able to bring that island into his domain as a protectorate when he made peace with the ruling chief, Kaumuali'i. Malo noted that Kamehameha had remembered Kūkona's sparing the captive chiefs' lives, and this is why Kamehameha spared Kaumuali'i's life when they met to negotiate a treaty.

Kamehameha's reign was one of peace, of laws to protect the defenseless and aged, and of righteous living that carefully balanced the increasing intrusion of foreigners and their ways with traditional life. That reign came to a traumatic end when Kamehameha died at Kailua-Kona on the morning of May 8, 1819.

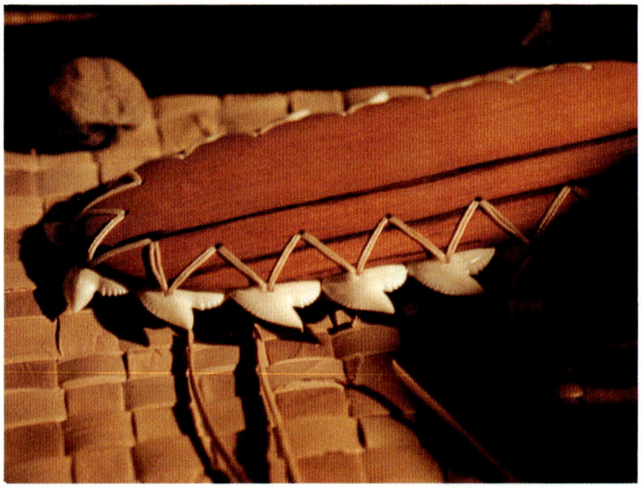

Following traditions, upon his death, the chiefs and people went into a state of mourning. As part of the mourning ceremonies to mark the death of a great chief there was a period of "free eating" of usually prohibited foods, to flout the former *kapu* [tabu] system of that chief and thereby establish a new order of his successor. Kamakau explains that after a period of mourning and of free eating, "the new ruler placed the land under a new tabu . . . the custom of the tabu upon free eating was kept up because . . . it was believed that the ruler who did not proclaim the tabu had not long to rule. If he attempted to continue the practice of free eating he was quickly disinherited. It was regarded as an impious act practiced by those alone who did not believe in a god."

At the time of Kamehameha's death, a great controversy developed. Kamehameha's oldest son and heir, Kalanikua Liholiho, who was with his cousin, Ka'owa Kekuaokalani, attending purification rites, had been asked to return to where the chiefs had gathered for the free eating. He refused, but Kamehameha's favorite wife, Ka'ahumanu, persisted, and Liholiho returned.

The next day Ka'ahumanu announced Kamehameha's final wishes. She arrived via canoe from the place of mourning to a beach where the chiefs were assembled. In the midst of great pageantry she disembarked from her canoe and proclaimed Kamehameha's eldest son, Liholiho, as Kamehameha II and that his rule would be shared with her as regent.

Another 19th-century historian and companion-guardian of the chiefs, John Papa 'Ī'ī, described the arrangements by which Kamehameha wished the rule to be continued by his sons by his wife Keōpūolani, a high ranking chiefess, and then by his grandsons. Kamehameha requested that his daughters by another wife marry his grandsons to continue his line.

This indicated that Kamehameha wanted to establish a dynasty not unlike the European monarchies that he became familiar with through conversations with captains and emissaries of visiting foreign ships. If this was Kamehameha's intent he complicated it by also taking a part from the story of 'Umi. Kamakau reported:

"While still in possession of all his faculties Kamehameha proclaimed Kalanikua Liholiho heir to the kingdom after his death, and he was given the tabu of the gods of the heiau [temple]. His god, Kūkā'ilimoku, Kamehameha gave to Ka'owa Kekuaokalani [Kamehameha's nephew]. These two, the kingdom and the god, were considered of equal importance in ancient days. So Līloa had passed the two down to his two sons, the kingdom to Hākau, the god to 'Umi, who however came into possession of the kingdom because the one to whom it was given failed to rule aright."

Certainly by establishing a dynastic succession Kamehameha was moving the chiefdom to become a monarchy. But, did he also intend by this re-enactment of the inheritance of the land and the god to give assurance that, if something went wrong, the traditional model of rule could be reinstated?

After the proclamation of succession, two of Kamehameha's wives began the process that would allow something to go wrong. Keōpūolani looked at her son, Liholiho, the new ruler, and put her hand to her mouth as a sign for free eating. Liholiho was very torn as to what to do, whether to join in this free eating and thereby break all tradition or to not to be a part of it.

He returned to the temple for prayers and remained there with his cousin, Kekuaokalani. Ka'ahumanu persisted again in sending messengers to get Liholiho's permission to declare a release from any further eating restrictions. And the "chief bent his head in reflection and then looked up and assented," Kamakau tells us. It appears that he reluctantly joined his mother and other female chiefs in this free eating. At that point, Ka'ahumanu then urged him, "Make eating free over the whole kingdom from Hawai'i to O'ahu and let it be extended to Kaua'i!" Liholiho consented.

When Kekuaokalani heard that Liholiho had proclaimed free eating for all the islands, Kamakau reports that "he was angry with Ka'ahumanu and the whole family of chiefs for forcing this upon the young *ali'i* [Liholiho, early twenties] and ending the tabu of the chiefs." Disgruntled, Kekuaokalani departed from them. Ka'ahumanu must have perceived this to be potentially dangerous, so she sent her cousin Kalanimoku and a party of warriors after Kekuaokalani to talk him into joining them. As the canoes were to depart, Keōpūolani decided to go with them. After several attempts to negotiate failed, Keōpūolani intervened and said to Kekuaokalani, "So you cut the navel cord, my brother, by this act." This meant his blood relationship was being severed, that he was being disowned.

The next day the loyalist forces led by Kalanimoku defeated the "rebels" of Kekuaokalani at the battle of Kuamo'o. His defeat signaled the end of the prohibitions on food and the silencing of those who wanted to keep the status quo of the chiefdom. It signaled the end of the *kapu* system, its temples and images, and the first rebellion against the Kamehameha dynasty.

The situation Kamehameha left behind was the result of a complex set of marriages and births that had evolved from a

King Tamaahamah
His X Mark

AT LEFT:

Kamehameha the Great sent a letter to King George III of England in 1810 during the Napoleonic Wars. Stiffly he conveyed this message, "Captain Vancouver said you would send me a small vessel. I am sorry to say I have not received one. Sorry to hear you are at war with so many powers and (I am) so far off and cannot assist you."

AT RIGHT:

Portrait of Queen Ka'ahumanu. Wood encased mirrors came with early trading ships. Kilo pōhaku are stone mirrors used by the Hawaiians. They were made of compact basalt from the base of Mauna Kea and placed in a shallow bowl of water. Feather lei is of 'ō'ō and 'apapane feathers. Bishop Museum Collection

KING KAMEHAMEHA II

1797 - 1824

In 1823, King Kamehameha II and his Queen, Kamāmalu, set sail for England with an entourage of high-born chiefs and chiefesses. The trip ended tragically when the king and queen, vulnerable to foreign diseases, were stricken fatally with the measles.

Rihoriho Iolani

In the 1820's, the islands were struggling through cultural chaos. The first Missionary Company arrived from New England amid public nudity, incest, murder, adultery, drunk-

common ancestry of a woman named Keakealaniwahine, and Kamehameha's desire to duplicate her rank and status in his children and grandchildren. The most desired children of chiefs were sacred children who were able to "return" to a state of being godlike through marriage between certain relatives, in what was known as an "arched" or "bridging" marriage. These were the children who were like gods; whose signs were the thunder, lightning, the rainbows and who conversed with chiefs and retainers only at night.

Keakealaniwahine was such a child. Unequaled in rank by any other chiefess, she became ruler of the island of Hawai'i, and was succeeded by her son. Kamehameha I was her great-great-grandson on his paternal side. His own grandparents were brother and sister, and his parents were cousins.

Kamehameha's favorite wife, Ka'ahumanu, was his niece, as her grandfather (Keōua Kupuapaikalani) was Kamehameha's father. The other powerful ranking wife, Keōpūolani, was like her ancestress, Keakealaniwahine. According to Kamakau, Keōpūolani was "the only remaining high tabu chiefess, [when she] gave up the tabu with the consent of all the chiefs, the tabu system fell."

Ka'ahumanu could be seen as representing the political power through her parents and their resources of land, materials for weapons and canoes, and manpower; Keōpūolani could be seen as the sacred wife who brought the heirs of Kamehameha the ultimate in rank and status.

In fact, it was Keōpūolani's father, Kiwala'ō, who was to have become the ruling chief of the island of Hawai'i after his father died. He was given the land and Kamehameha was given the war god. He became an obstacle to Kamehameha's desire to unite the island of Hawai'i. Kiwala'ō was killed at a crucial battle by none other than Ka'ahumanu's father, Ke'eaumoku Pāpa'iaheahe.

Furthermore, it was Ka'ahumanu's father who warned Kamehameha that the only person who truly threatened his rule was his own daughter. He indicated to Kamehameha that Ka'ahumanu was the real "rebel" and that if he wanted to see his rule last beyond himself, then he had to secure her from all others.

Kamakau reaffirms that the marriage between Kamehameha and Ka'ahumanu was an "alliance" in which "Kamehameha's long control of the government was due to this wife alone; through her all the chiefs became reconciled to Kamehameha."

If the three cousins of the same generation, Keōpūolani, Ka'ahumanu and Kalanimoku, were to fulfill Kamehameha's wishes, then the destruction of the *kapu* system, the temples and images was inevitable.

If they wanted to suppress any rebellion or rival family claims that had so plagued the rule of other chiefs and to ensure that a dynasty of the Kamehamehas would succeed, then the system which gave credibility to those claims had to be ended. The chiefdom was changing into a kingdom and the rules had to change, too.

Continued on page 52

Queen Kamāmalu

enness and prostitution. In their attempt to Christianize the "heathen natives" singing was made a punishable offense, dancing the hula was condemned, horseback riding on Sunday tabooed. It was also during this time that British Consul Richard Charlton left a mission school after he had "with his own eyes seen four couples fornicating during prayers." Sex was far removed from sin or evil to the native Hawaiian who viewed it as life's most natural pleasure. An islander's hospitality might be extended by offering his wife or daughter in an act of friendship. Refusal was considered rude.

Nāhi'ena'ena

Kauikeaouli

Love, Trapped Between Cultures

They were kapu children of Kamehameha I caught in the interface of changing customs and beliefs. In the tradition of their ancestors, the ideal union of a chief of the highest rank was with his sister, also of high rank. A union of this kind would produce the most sacred children. The children's mother Keōpūolani was of even higher rank than her husband. It was she who was the first to be baptized and given a Christian name. It was her children who were the first to be taught the missionaries' letters. The young boy Kauikeaouli became Kamehameha III at the age of ten when his brother died of measles in London. Their sister Nāhi'ena'ena was placed under the guardianship of Rev. William Richardson who instilled in her the fear of God. Like her mother, she was baptized and took the Christian name, Harriet.

Queen Kalama

Kamehameha III
Kauikeaouli

A growing love relationship between brother and sister horrified the missionaries who did what they could to keep them apart and teach them the evils of their incestuous ways. Sometimes as Nāhi'ena'ena, the kapu chiefess, and other times as Harriet, a devoted student of the Bible, there was no harmony, compromise or peace in the young woman's life. She died after childbirth with a torn heart and shattered spirits on December 30, 1836 at the young age of 21. Kauikeaouli wailed for the love of his sister and moved his residence to be near her burial site. With devotion he built her a mausoleum in Maui and made the day of her death a public observance. The experience leading to her death chastened the young king who had been leading a life in pursuance of pleasures. He gave up drinking, shut down his distilleries, and outlawed importing spirits. Pressured to perpetuate the race, he married Kalama Ka-paku-haili on February 14, 1837. Unfortunately, this marriage did not produce a royal heir.

An interesting story about Queen Kalama tells of her attempt to swim from Hawai'i to Australia, but she gave it up when she realized how far this was. It seems the queen was bored and thought she might break the all time distance record.

Kamehameha III

1813 - 1854

Ruled from June 6, 1824 to December 15, 1854

In the time of Kamehameha III, Herman Melville was to write, "Civilization has scattered her vices and withheld her blessings".

In his youth, the king pursued wild pleasures. With maturity he proved to be an able monarch. He was beloved by his people and highly regarded by the foreign residents. The U.S. Commissioner to the islands, David L. Gregg said of him, "...good looking, shrewd, and far more intelligent about political affairs than might be expected from one just emerged from a savage state. He would by no means disgrace the society of his brother monarches in Europe and I am very much disposed to think that in part of natural capacity, he is superior to them all except Nicholas and Louis Napoleon."

Royal patent document, agricultural medal, uniform buttons. Don Medcalf Collection

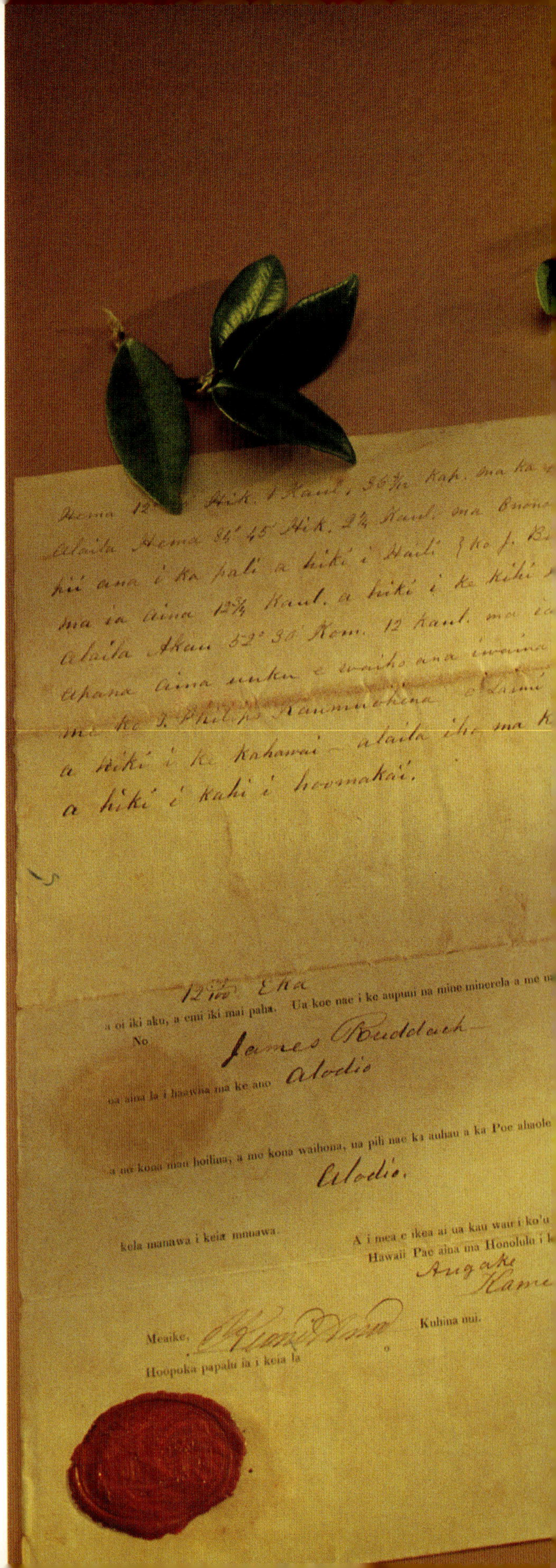

No. 38
ROYAL PATEN
UPON CONFIRMATION OF THE
WHEREAS, the Board of Commissioners to quiet Land
James Ruddach
estate in Fee Simple in the
and hereafter described
Therefore, Kamehameha, by the grace of God, King of the Hawaiian Islands, by this royal patent
makes known unto all men, that he has for himself and his successors in office, this day granted and given
Absolutely in Fee Simple
unto the said James Ruddach
all that certain piece of land situate at Laimi - Nuuanu Valley in the
Island of Oahu and described by
boundaries as follows.
Commencing at Rock marked + on W. edge
of Nuuanu River joining Kawaiolena (A. Paki) and
running S. 70° 45' W. 52 8/10 ft. up to stake on top of
River Bank (near Ruddachs House) Thence N. 45°
West 5 ch. 21 1/10 feet along row of hau trees
road - thence along Makai to Ononokoiniu
Stone wall - Thence S. 43° E. 8 Ch. 15 8/10 ft.
Ononokoiniu to angle of wall; Thence
1 Chain 44 1/10 ft. to angle of Wall; Thence
42 8/10 ft. to angle of wall; Thence S.
35 8/10 ft. to Bank of river; Thence S.
21 1/10 feet across River to angle
E. 1 Ch. 36 8/10 feet along wall to angle;
S. 84° 45' E. 2 1/4 ch. up pali always along
Koinui to J. Booths (Heiili) Thence along
Heiili 12 3/4 Ch. to E. corner of this; Thence
N. 52° 30' W. 12 ch. along small piece of land between
KAMEHAMEHA

Height from ridge to first projection 12 ft

Projection 16 inches 2nd do 10 in

			ft in
Turrets 2 feet wide		4 / 2	8
Space 2 ft 6 in	2 6 / 3 / 7.6		7.6 / 15.6

Width of front of tower —— 15 ft 6 in

Height of turrets 2 feet to cap.

AT LEFT:

The plans and elevation of Kawaiaha'o Church, by Reverend Hiram Bingham, represents the earliest Hawaiian architectural drawings known.

ABOVE:

The coral block building was completed in 1842 replacing the grassy house of worship before it. Reverend Bingham dominated the mission for twenty years before returning to New England when his wife took ill. From his writings, we know that he never gave up hope to return to the islands. Unfortunately, he never saw the islands again but the solid new church fulfilled his dreams and served the congregation well. Photos courtesy Hawaiian Historical Society

ABOVE:
"A signature of a stranger from the Hawaiian islands", Kamehameha V (Prince Lot, 1850). Don Medcalf Collection

OPPOSITE:
Alexander Liholiho's journal 1849 - 1850 recording the daily events of his trip to England, Paris, Washington D.C., and New York City. Courtesy Hawaiian Historical Society

Prince Alexander Liholiho and his brother Prince Lot accompanied Dr. Gerrit P. Judd on a diplomatic journey to Europe and America in the years 1849 - 1850. The experience forever set his admiration for English institutions, European tastes, and distaste for Americans. Mistaken for a Negro on a train in Washington, D.C., he recorded the unfortunate experience in his daily journal, " I took hold of his arm, and asked him his reasons, and what right he had in turning me out and talking to me in the way he did...I found he was the conductor, and probably had taken me for somebody's servant, just because I had a darker skin than he had. Confounded fool!" Five years after this incident he would become Kamehameha IV. His attitude towards Americans was tainted for the rest of his life affecting island politics for years to come. Prince Lot took the throne as Kamehameha V after the death of his brother.

Alexander Scholiko's Private Journal.
1849

OPPOSITE:

Queen Emma and Kamehameha IV portraits. In Emma's hand and in the foreground is a miniature bouquet holder, a wedding gift from her husband, Kamehameha IV. The cabinet with convex and concave glass panels was made in Germany for the queen with koa wood sent from Hawai'i. The china was a gift to the royal couple from Queen Victoria. Photographed at Queen Emma Summer Palace, courtesy of Daughters of Hawai'i

KAMEHAMEHA IV

Alexander Liholiho

1834 - 1863

Ruled from December 15, 1854 to November 30, 1863

***H**is manner and style was very English but his volatile temper was definitely the mark of a Kamehameha.*

Alexander Liholiho (King Kamehameha IV) and Queen Emma were both well educated and took an active interest in the arts. Their court was run with elegance and grace. He loved horseback riding and a good game of cricket. Together they entertained by presenting musicals and operas and, at times, even took to the stage for their aristocratic guests.

The king was a dichotomy displaying intelligence and logic but, at other times, he was irrational and driven by emotion. In an act of jealousy, after a long day of drinking, he shot and critically wounded his friend and secretary Henry Neilson who was suspected of having an affair with Emma. The rumor proved to be unfounded and the young king never recovered from the anguish of his deed. He is remembered for founding the Queen's Hospital with Emma and establishing the Anglican Church in Hawai'i.

PRINCE ALBERT EDWARD KAUIKEAOULI LEIOPAPA A KAMEHAMEHA

The Little Prince

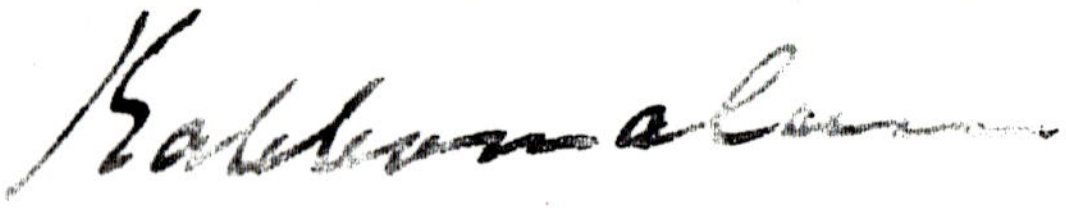

***T**he son of Queen Emma and King Kamehameha IV was the joy of his parents and the treasure of the Hawaiian Kingdom. With him laid the promise of the perpetuation of the Kamehameha dynasty.*

The little prince at age 4 had a temper tantrum over a pair of boots. To cool his uncontrollable fit, his father put the child's head under a faucet of cold water. Later that day Prince Albert lapsed into nervous weeping, then developed brain fever and never recovered from the shock. The grief over the loss of the "Son of the Nation" was immeasurable. The king was already suffering from asthma and nerve disorders. His poor health coupled with his anguish over the Neilson shooting and the loss of his son brought an early death on November 30, 1863, a year and three months after the death of his son.

After the death of the prince, the king bestowed upon the mourning queen the name Kaleleokalani (the flight of the heavenly chief). When the king died, Queen Emma changed it to the plural, Kaleleonālani (the flight of the heavenly chiefs). Prince Albert's boot and brown velvet jacket, Queen Emma Summer Palace, courtesy Daughters of Hawai'i

Diamond Head 1857

by G.H. Burgess.

A view from Honolulu Beach.

David Cornwell Collection

HER ROYAL HIGHNESS

Princess Ruth Keelikolani

Requests the pleasure of your company at a

LUAU,

AT HER RESIDENCE,

KAAKOPUA, EMMA STREET, HONOLULU.

On Thursday, February 9, 1882.

FROM 12 TO 2 O'CLOCK

"Keōua Hale." Two lavish lū'au and a grand ball were planned to celebrate the completion of Princess Ruth Ke'elikōlani's new home. Photos: Hawaiian Historical Society

THE HOUSE THAT RUTH BUILT

She was grand in enormous proportions. Big hearted, generous and ferociously proud of her heritage, Princess Ruth Ke'elikōlani, one of the last Kamehamehas, was not a woman to be outdone by anyone. Her Victorian mansion was planned to be the most magnificent house in the islands. The princess, however, was never to enjoy her new home. She fell ill the day after her gala house-warming celebration and choose to spend her remaining days in the style of her ancestors, dying in the home of her heart, a grass house in Kailua, Kona, leaving her entire estate to her cousin, Bernice Pauahi Bishop.

Bernice Pauahi Bishop refused the crown but dedicated her life to serving her people with kindness and generosity. Her final will and testament is a reflection of her vision and compassion. The income of her lands was used to establish, and maintains to this day, Kamehameha Schools, a school for students of Hawaiian ancestry.

AT RIGHT:

Photograph of Bernice Pauahi Bishop and "invitation to a fancy party" from the Bishops to the Cleghorns. Don Medcalf Collection

Mr & Mrs Bishop
request the pleasure of
Calico Party
the 6th October at
Sept 20th
Costume

Kamehameha's final wishes had been kept by his favorite wives and their families, and in doing so they created a kingdom for his sons and grandsons to inherit. Native historian Kamakau would later comment:

"Some people say that the Kamehamehas won the kingdom through successful warfare ... The chiefs disputed about the succession while Kamehameha was living, and Kamehameha asked the opinion of men skilled in genealogies and of the orators and those who knew about the government in ancient days. Some of the chiefs and governors thought that the old standards should not count in succession. But the skilled men told Kamehameha that in order to keep the kingdom united as he left it and prevent its falling to pieces at his death, he must consolidate it under one ruler and must leave it to an heir who was in the ruling line from his ancestors. He should therefore appoint Liholiho his heir and his younger brother, Kau-i-ke-aouli, to succeed him ... The inheriting of the kingdom by these two chiefs put an end to rebellious thoughts and gave peace to the country."

After a reign of five years, Liholiho, Kamehameha II, would die while visiting Great Britain, the very country of the first foreign explorer to reach Hawai'i, Captain James Cook.

Kauikeaouli, King Kamehameha III, would have the longest reign of any of the Hawaiian monarchs. He was the first of the monarchs to use the term "king," as foreign influences began to induce great changes in island society. His reign witnessed the next fundamental changes of governance in the islands: the establishment of a constitutional monarchy; the development of laws, law enforcement and judicial process; the division of lands for ownership, including acknowledgment of the rights of ordinary citizens to own land; and the acceptance of Christianity. He proclaimed that his kingdom "shall be a kingdom of learning" and said, "I give my kingdom to God." This was a period of enlightenment in which Kamakau would boast that Hawai'i was ahead of the enlightened countries of Europe in literacy.

Kauikeaouli, whose own children died in infancy, adopted his nephew, a grandson of Kamehameha I, Alexander Liholiho, as his son, thereby providing an heir from the line of the ruling family. Upon Kauikeaouli's death, which ended a reign of 21 years, Alexander Liholiho became Kamehameha IV. His reign continued the further urbanization and economic development of the islands.

Alexander Liholiho strived to maintain the precarious balance of power that the tiny kingdom had among the many foreign countries, recalling the words of native scholar Davida Malo, who wrote, "The ships of the foreigners have come and smart people have arrived from the large nations ... they know our people are few and living in a small nation; they will eat us up, such has always been the case with large nations, the small ones have been gobbled up."

Kamehameha IV died at the age of 29, after the tragic death of his four-year-old son, Albert Edward Kauikeaouli LeioPapa a Kamehameha, the "prince of Hawai'i," and the last infant to be born of the Kamehamehas. Alexander Liholiho's reign lasted a few days short of nine years. His older brother, Lot Kapuāiwa, succeeded him as Kamehameha V.

One of the first acts of the new king was to refuse to take the oath to support the constitution of his uncle, King Kamehameha III. Wanting to restore the authority of the Crown, Kamehameha V convened a constitutional convention and when the delegates could not reach agreement, he dismissed them. It was his wish "to maintain the kingdom as an independent monarchy," for other Pacific islands, such as Tahiti and New Zealand, were now under foreign control.

His reign of nine years saw the continued growth of the sugar industry and major capital developments, such as a new post office building, and a hotel to accommodate the many overseas visitors arriving on the passenger steamships in port.

Kamehameha V died on his 42nd birthday, December 11, 1872, and being a bachelor, he had no heirs. The king's half-sister, Ruth Ke'elikōlani, was the sole heir to his estate, but she and Bernice Pauahi Bishop, the other surviving grandchild of Kamehameha I, had no interest in occupying the throne. The reign of the Kamehameha dynasty had lasted for nearly 80 years.

In the absence of a successor to the throne, the Hawaiian Constitution provided that the Legislature elect the next monarch from among the highest-ranking chiefs. William Lunalilo was elected as the new king. His mother was a niece and wife of Kamehameha I, and she served as *kuhina nui*, premier, under Kamehameha III. King Lunalilo's reign lasted only a brief year; he died on February 3, 1874.

Like Kamehameha V, Lunalilo had no heir and had not named a successor, so the Legislature held another election. In a hotly contested election, David Kalākaua defeated the rival candidate, the dowager Queen Emma, widow of Kamehameha IV and a great-granddaughter of Kamehameha I's brother, Keli'imaika'i. Upon hearing the results of the election, Queen Emma's supporters rioted.

King Kalākaua's ancestors were chiefs who had aided and supported Kamehameha I in his quest to unify the islands. Kalākaua established his own dynasty when he made his brother, William Pitt Leleiōhoku II, the heir to the throne.

Kalākaua's reign was one of grandiose visions to ensure the kingdom's place in the world. He was the first monarch to travel around the world, and with controversial advisors Kalākaua sought to form alliances in the Pacific region. He also had to ensure the kingdom's economic growth vested in the sugar industry by seeking favorable tariffs with the United States, the islands' largest and closest trading partner.

In domestic politics Kalākaua had to balance the interests of the Native Hawaiians and the interests of a small, powerful and vocal business community composed of men of American and European birth or ancestry. It was not an easy task, particularly to secure revenues to cover all these concerns.

The day came when that business community was strong enough to accuse the king of corruption, patronage and bribery and, backed by a large and well organized volunteer militia, in 1887 they forced the king to dismiss his own cabinet and accept a new constitution. Dubbed the "Bayonet Constitution," it greatly limited his powers, and reduced the Native Hawaiians' voting rights and elected representation, while increasing the powers of foreigners to vote and to hold office.

A few years later, King Kalākaua left for California to rest, citing ill health. He died in San Francisco on January 20, 1891. Citizens in Honolulu waited for his return, not knowing of

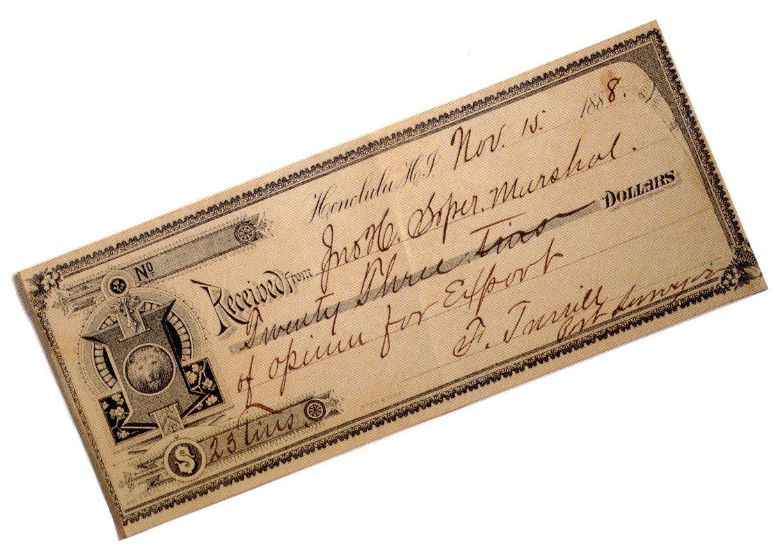
Honolulu H.I. Nov. 15 1888.

No

Received from Jno H. Soper. Marshal.

Twenty Three tins DOLLARS

of opium for Export

F. Turrill

$ 23 tins

his death. When the ship carrying his remains arrived, their planned welcome turned into mourning and laments.

Following the earlier, untimely death of Prince Leleiōhoku, Kalākaua had named his younger sister, Princess Lydia Liliʻuokalani, as heir to the throne. She became Queen Liliʻuokalani, the kingdom's first and last ruling queen. She named as her successor her niece, Princess Kaʻiulani.

Neither Queen Liliʻuokalani nor the Native Hawaiian population accepted the forced Bayonet Constitution imposed on her brother, which had never been brought to popular vote. She wished to proclaim a new constitution to restore the Crown's authority and the Native Hawaiians' rights. She chose Saturday, January 14, 1893, as her opportunity to do so.

She had received numerous petitions and delegations from Native Hawaiian subjects requesting a new constitution; an opposition cabinet had just been voted out of office by a coalition of native parties, and the Legislature, which was empowered to initiate the process for a constitutional convention, ended January 14.

At the close of the Legislature, the Royal Hawaiian Band played as Liliʻuokalani left the Legislature building, Aliʻiōlani Hale, through the royal entrance behind the statue of King Kamehameha I. She returned to ʻIolani Palace, where members of the Native Hawaiian political parties, members of the Legislature, judges and guests began arriving to hear her proclaim their new constitution. They joined the queen's ladies-in-waiting inside the Throne Room. It was a little after the noon hour, and the arriving guests added to the sense of anticipation and excitement.

A large crowd of Hawaiians also assembled outside, standing on the palace grounds. Unbeknown to them, Liliʻuokalani was meeting with her cabinet ministers to ask for their support and signatures for the new constitution. What she did not anticipate on that day was their reluctance and timidity to sidestep the constitutional process, as written in the Bayonet Constitution, for loyalty to their queen. Unlike Kamehameha V, she truly believed that she needed her cabinet's approval of her actions. Concerned that her enemies would seize this opportunity to challenge her, the Cabinet persuaded her to defer proclaiming a new constitution.

It was getting into the late afternoon, past the heat of the day, but the scores of people remained waiting to hear word from their queen. Liliʻuokalani entered the Throne Room and told those gathered there, "I have prepared and have expected to promulgate a new constitution today, for this is the proper time, and in that way the desires of my beloved subjects will be met. But with great regret I reveal to you that I have met with resistance. Return to your homes in peace and without any disturbances. Please continue to regard me with such respect as I regard you. Let me be steadfast in your affection. I have been invited to postpone submission of the constitution for some other appropriate time. I must discuss it with my Cabinet ... You are uppermost in my love and I am sad to have to dismiss you."

Those gathered in the Throne Room responded with praise for the queen, assuring her of their devotion and that they would wait patiently until such time as their wishes would be fulfilled. After conveying her love, she left the room.

A few moments later she stood on the upper balcony of the palace and spoke to the crowd amassed on the grounds. She

Kamehameha V

Lot Kapuāiwa

1830 - 1872

Ruled from November 30, 1863 to December 11, 1872

Kamehameha V initiated numerous building projects including the Hawaiian Hotel, the first upscale hotel in the islands; 'Iolani Barracks, headquarters for the royal household guards; Ali'iōlani Hale, "House of the Chief Unto Heaven"; and a new prison and schoolhouses. Kamehameha IV designed Ali'iōlani Hale to be the new royal palace but delays and insufficient finances kept him from seeing its completion. The kingdom's strained budget dictated that the building have a more practical usage. It became the Government Office Building.

ABOVE:

Photo of Ali'iōlani Hale from Queen Street entrance.

Hawai'i State Archives

assured them that at the proper time in the future she would carry out their wishes and they would have a new constitution. Hearing this, they gave her loud cheers.

Leaked reports of the queen's initial plans by her own ministers gave the minority business community a chance to organize and for some of its more radical members to act upon their desired dream of annexation to the United States. They declared the queen's actions were "revolutionary acts" that menaced the public safety with "threats of violence and bloodshed from those with whom she was acting."

Although Lili'uokalani and her Cabinet ministers issued a proclamation upholding the constitutional process and deferring the new constitution, a group of businessmen formed a Committee of Safety to plan the overthrow of the monarchy. They drafted a letter to the U.S. Minister in Hawai'i, John Stevens, who was an avowed annexationist. It read, "We are unable to protect ourselves without the aid, and therefore, pray for the protection of the United States forces." The letter was signed by six subjects of the kingdom, who were either naturalized citizens or Hawai'i-born of foreign (mainly American) ancestry, and by five Americans, one British and one German citizen.

On the afternoon of January 16, after failed attempts by the Cabinet to talk with the U.S. minister, 162 armed American troops disembarked from the USS *Boston,* which was anchored in the harbor, and marched through downtown Honolulu. They landed without permission of the kingdom, and they were stationed 200 yards from the palace itself. The governor of O'ahu and the minister of foreign affairs for the kingdom immediately filed protests with U.S. Minister Stevens.

The next day, in the early afternoon, the Committee of Safety members, having drafted a proclamation ending the monarchy, left the safety of their armory building to take over the government building, Ali'iōlani Hale. As they were on their way, a policeman was shot near Fort Street while attempting to stop a delivery of ammunition to the armory. During the disturbance, the committee members reached the government building undetected and read their proclamation establishing a provisional government. They read it from the steps of the public entrance to that building, the opposite side from where, just three days before, Lili'uokalani had departed from the closing of the Legislature to the sounds of the Royal Hawaiian Band. There were no royal troops guarding the building, and only a few clerks were in the offices since the Legislature had ended.

Throughout the day, the queen had sent official messages to the U.S. minister assuring him of her support for the constitutional process and seeking his assurance of assistance to maintain the monarchy against armed insurrection. But as soon as the leaders of the overthrow read their proclamation, he prematurely recognized the provisional government as the existing government of the islands.

As evening approached in the palace, Lili'uokalani met with her Cabinet, two advisory council members and prominent loyal citizens. They advised her to surrender under protest to the U.S. forces. They argued that those forces were far superior and that the troops were in collusion with the U.S. minister in aiding the revolutionaries of the provisional

Prince Consort
John Owen Dominis
Husband of Lili'uokalani
(1840 - 1891)

government. Their mere presence so close to the palace and so far away from the American properties, which they supposedly had come ashore to protect, was intimidating and provocative. The royalists stated to the queen that "we would have to fight a great nation like the United States with her millions of men, and to do this would cause the sacrifice of hundreds of valuable human lives." And they reasoned that by surrendering to the United States of America the queen would be entitled to present her case to that government for arbitration. Lili'uokalani seemed resigned to these conclusions.

Between 6 and 7 o'clock, the corner of time in which the world of daylight, of human order, turned to become the darkness of night, the time of the spirits and gods, Queen Lili'uokalani signed a letter of surrender. She stated that, in order to prevent loss of lives, she was yielding, under protest, to "the superior force of the United States of America." She expressed her belief that, when given the facts, the United States government would "undo the action of its representative and reinstate me in the authority which I claim as the constitutional sovereign of the Hawaiian Islands."

"We were all stunned," wrote Bernice Pi'ilani Irwin, a supporter of the queen, in her memoirs. "I went around in a daze. I felt it must all be a tragic mistake, a nightmare from which we would all soon awaken. The sweet face of the queen seemed to haunt me. I pictured her as she always looked when she greeted me with her gentle smile, and I recalled all the kindnesses she had shown our family. I could not bear to think of her having this ignominy thrust upon her. My heart grieved for her."

There was no resistance by the Native Hawaiian population. Lili'uokalani and Hawaiian leaders had urged the people to remain calm and patient while awaiting a decision from the United States government, with faith in the expectation of justice.

Under the darkness of night the palace lamps glowed and flickered upon the walls. Most of those who came to give advice and to console the queen would quietly leave the palace grounds. The next morning, at the request of the provisional government, the queen left the palace for Washington Place, her private residence. The flag of the Hawaiian Kingdom flew no more.

If the kingdom officially ceased to exist, it did not in the hearts of the Native Hawaiian population. It continued on, wrote Bernice Irwin, as the "streets were filled with men wearing hatbands inscribed *Aloha 'Āina* (Love of Country). Hawaiian women busied themselves making flag patterned bed quilts while men fashioned shields of *koa* wood, painting them with the Hawaiian coat-of-arms surmounted by crossed Hawaiian flags in order to keep their beloved emblem constantly before their eyes." *Aloha 'Āina.*

MAI POINA OE IA'U

In 1895 Lili'uokalani was arrested and tried for treason. While she was kept imprisoned in the 'Iolani Palace she signed satin ribbons and gave them to her supporters. "Mai Poina 'Oe Ia'u" it implored. Do not forget me.

KING LUNALILO

William C. Lunalilo

1835 - 1874

Ruled from January 8, 1873 to February 3, 1874

He was so loved and regarded he became known as the "People's King." Testament to his commitment to caring for the health and welfare of his people, Lunalilo's will dictated that the proceeds of the sale of his estate would go to creating a home for aged Hawaiians.

Lunalilo.

Photographs

Kalakaua Rex.

KING KALĀKAUA

1836-1891

Ruled from February 12, 1874 to January 20, 1891

David Kalākaua, supporter of "Hawai'i for Hawaiians", accepted his earlier defeat to Lunalilo with dignity but procured his ambition to be king ever onward. The day after the death of King Lunalilo, Kalākaua threw his name in the hat and stepped forward to claim his destiny. It was, however, not without a fight. The dowager Queen Emma waged an aggressive campaign passing out handbills in English and Hawaiian, fueling a furious propaganda war to the end. On February 12, 1884, the Legislature convened for the election, each legislator receiving two ballots, a plain one for Queen Emma and one with a black heart for Kalākaua.

While many Americans did not trust Kalākaua, his opponent was distinctly pro British. Supporting Kalākaua therefore would seemingly be in their best interest. The announcement of Kalākaua's victory touched off angry native mobs which required American and British forces to restore order. Peace restored, Kalākaua took his oath of office. Emma sent him a message acknowledging him as sovereign and retired from politics.

ABOVE:

'Iolani Palace

AT RIGHT:

Kalākaua election medal, silver, gold, enamel. The mōʻī (king) medal which commemorated Kalākaua's election victory was awarded to special supporters. The heart was the emblem used on his ballot. It bears the initials of the king. Considered rare. Don Medcalf Collection

ABOVE:

Kamehameha Day at the races...

The Hawaiian Jockey Club's popular annual event at Kapi'olani Park. Admission was a dollar and an additional fifty cents was charged to those who came on horseback. Photo: David Cornwell Collection.

RIGHT:

Race program, 1885, Hawaiian Historical Society

Second Annual Race Meeting

OF THE

HAWAIIAN JOCKEY CLUB

KAMEHAMEHA DAY

RACE PROGRAMME

KAPIOLANI PARK

JUNE 11th, 1885

RACES COMMENCE 10.30 O'CLOCK SHARP.

KŪMĀKENA

"Wailing for the dead..."

The death march of the passing ali'i was swift and seemingly never ending. The lives of the royal families were short and all too often, childless. The last of the Kamehamehas died in rapid succession: Princess Ruth in 1883, Bernice Pauahi Bishop in 1884, Queen Emma in 1885. In 1887 King Kalākaua's sister Princess Likelike passed on as did Prince Edward at age 18. Kalākaua's brother and heir apparent, Leleiōhoku, died when he was 22. Princess Ka'iulani, also groomed to rule, died at age 24.

W. Leleiohoku

FROM TOP LEFT:
Princess Ka'iulani circa 1897, Princess Ka'iulani childhood photo, her mother Likelike, her father Archibald Cleghorn, bottom: David Kawānanakoa, Leleiōhoku

Ainahau was the name of the grand estate Archibald Cleghorn built for his family. The land was a gift to his daughter Ka'iulani from her godmother Princess Ruth. Cleghorn cultivated the ten Waikīkī acres creating the most majestic garden. Upon his death, Cleghorn bequeathed the property to the Territory for use as a park. The legislature did not accept this gift and the estate was eventually demolished.

ABOVE:

Entryway to Āinahau.

David Cornwell Collection.

AT LEFT:

Letter of acceptance in response to an invitation to a ball at the ʻIolani Palace.

Don Medcalf Collection

"...Thus sweet memories come back to me
Bringing fresh remembrances of the heart
Dearest one, yes, thou art my own,
From thee true love shall ne'er depart.

I have seen and watched thy loveliness
Thou sweet rose of Maunawili
And 'tis there the birds oft love to dwell
And sip the honey from thy lips.

Farewell to thee, farewell to thee
Thou charming one who dwell in shaded bowers
One fond embrace e'er I depart
Until we meet again."

from "Aloha 'Oe"

Liliuokalani

Lili'uokalani, 1877

"Last night I had a vision
'Twas near the mid of night
It was thee in thy beauty
With a crown of sweet rose-buds.

Whilst in my dreams enchanted
By guitars charming strains,
With the sweet voice of my jewel,
My gem, my diamond star."

"A Wreath from My Beloved"
from a song by Likelike

AT LEFT:
Princess Likelike.

AT RIGHT:
Her daughter Princess Ka'iulani and her address book, addresses of friends in London and a keepsake from a carriage drive at Versailles.
Don Medcalf Collection

GAZE'S HIGH-CLASS FOUR-IN-HAND
Drives
THE SIGHTS OF PARIS
VERSAILLES
Excursions to FONTAINEBLEAU
FIRMIN & SONS

ABOVE:
The uniform of Captain Robert Waipā Parker, head of the Palace Guards under both King Kalākaua and Queen Lili'uokalani. Courtesy of Paul Kauali'i and Margaret Lemn Parker

AT RIGHT:
Broadsides (bulletins) "Rally for reform" in English and Hawaiian. Signs of unrest and dissension preceding the general election on February 5, 1890, were the result of differences regarding constitutional changes and foreign policy. Hawaiian Historical Society

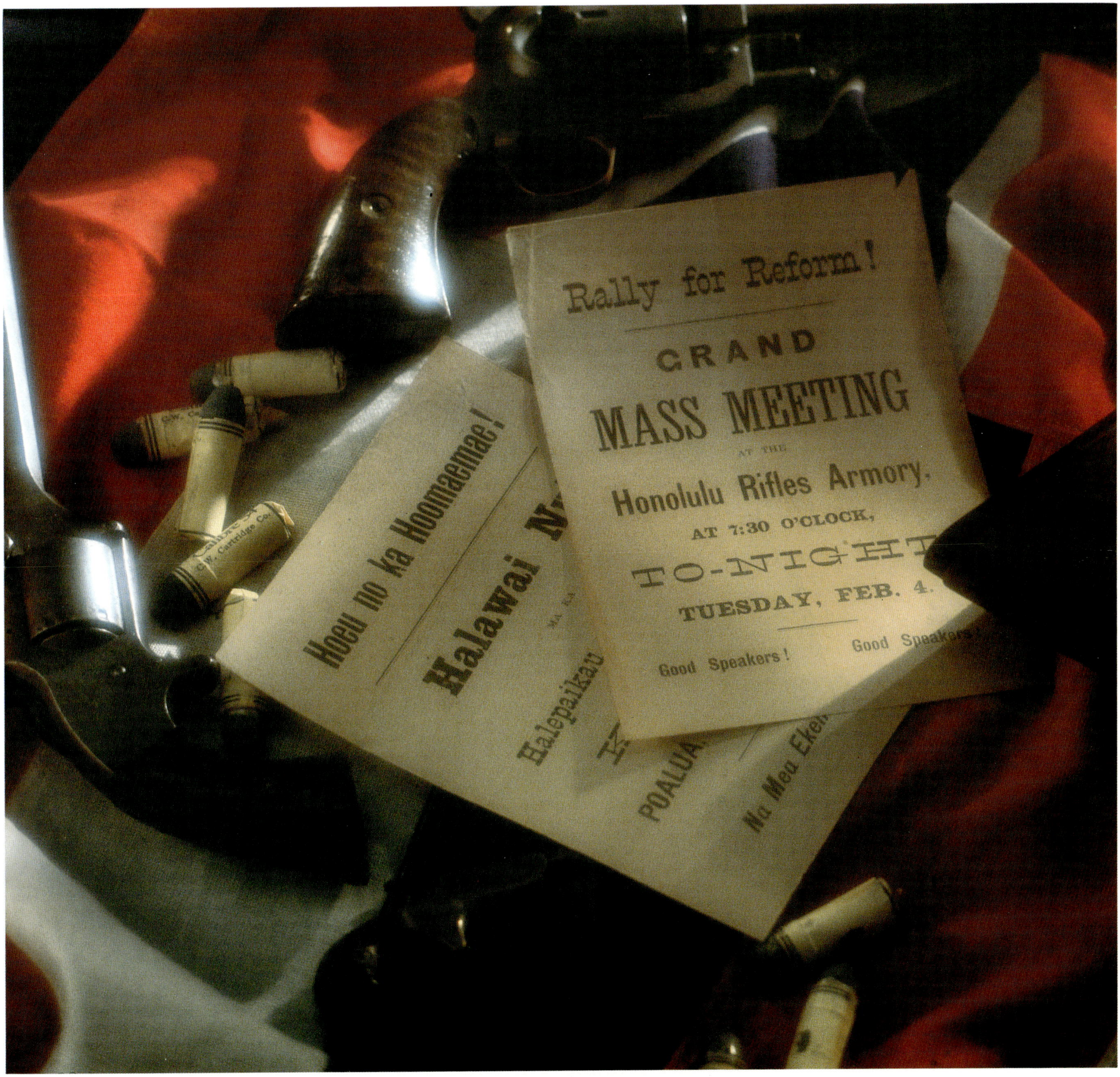

Rally for Reform!

GRAND

MASS MEETING

AT THE

Honolulu Rifles Armory,

AT 7:30 O'CLOCK,

TO-NIGHT

TUESDAY, FEB. 4.

Good Speakers! Good Speakers!

Hoeu no ka Hoomaemae!

Halepaikau

On August 12, 1898, the final transfer of sovereignty took place with a flag changing ceremony. Hawai'i's ali'i were invited but chose not to attend. They gathered, instead, at Lili'uokalani's residence in somber silence.
The invitation read:
"The Minister of Foreign Affairs invites Princess Ka'iulani to be present at the Ceremony attending the Transfer of the Sovereignty of the Republic of Hawaii to the United States of America, at the Executive Building at half after eleven, Friday morning, August 12, 1898."
Princess Ka'iulani's father, Archibald Cleghorn, responded to the invitation by begging to say that he and the Princess will necessarily have to decline. Dated August 11, 1898.

Invitation and letter, Don Medcalf Collection
RIGHT:
Ka'iulani photo, Grandy Keali'iho'okano Perry Collection

The Minister of Foreign Affairs
invites the Princess Kaiulani
to be present at the Ceremony
attending the Transfer of the
Sovereignty of the Republic of Hawaii
to the
United States of America
at the Executive Building
at half after eleven
Friday morning, August 12th
1898.

ABOVE:
Chief Kana'ina and his son William Charles Lunalilo circa 1850. In 1873, after the death of Kamehameha V, Lunalilo became Hawai'i's first elected king. Bishop Museum Archives

Lunalilo's last wish was to be buried away from the Kamehameha family at the Royal Mausoleum. He and his family felt slighted by the Kamehamehas so after his death, while his body waited at the Mausoleum, a tomb was built for him at the corner of the cemetery at Kawaiaha'o Church. When the tomb was ready, Chief Charles Kana'ina requested permission from King Kalākaua for a second twenty-one gun salute for his son as they lay his body in its final resting place. His request was denied. Angered, the chief stormed out of the palace saying the matter would be put into the hands of the gods. Indeed, it seems the gods granted his wish for on the day of the royal burial, it is recorded that the heavens opened with a crash of twenty-one claps of thunder and twenty-one bolts of lightning. It rained so hard for days after, ducks were sighted swimming in the flooded water around Kawaiaha'o Church in downtown Honolulu.

Lunalilo Mausoleum

Harbingers of aloha
Through a black lace veil, shimmering
Unlock our love,
Lest we forget from whence we came.

And as we too slip the surly bonds of earth,
To fly with ʻIwalani,
Let our children join hands here
To touch the soul of aloha.

Kawānanakoa gate inscription at the Royal Mausoleum

ABOVE:

Royal Mausoleum, Centennial Observance, January 17, 1993.

THE MORNING STAR ALONE KNOWS...

The burial spot of the bones of King Kamehameha I remains a mystery till today, but the members of the Kamehameha and Kalākaua dynasties are buried at the Royal Mausoleum in Nu'uanu Valley. King Lunalilo's last wish was to be buried away from the Kamehameha clan. His remains are near his family at Kawaiaha'o Church.

ABOVE:
*Hawai'i coat of arms,
Royal Mausoleum entry gate.*

Kamehameha Tomb

Ho'onani

to Adorn

CHAPTER TWO

In the traditions about ʻUmi, his mother was able to have her lover, the high chief Līloa, acknowledge ʻUmi as his legitimate son by receiving his *malo* (loincloth), *niho palaoa* (whale's tooth pendant) and his war club. Those were the signs by which Līloa would recognize ʻUmi was indeed his own son. They were the insignia that physically separated the *aliʻi* (chiefs) and *koa* (warriors) from the *kānaka* (people).

Among the many articles made in traditional society, there were specifically several that only those of rank and status could possess. These were the *niho palaoa, hulu manu* (feathers), *ʻaha ʻula* (sacred cordage), *pūloʻuloʻu* (signs of *kapu* or tabu), *kāhili* (feather standards), *kāʻei malo* (feather *malo*), *mahiole* (feather helmets), *ʻahu ʻula* (feather cloaks or capes), *hulikua* (feather leis or wreaths). The only others who could wear these articles or be adorned with them were the gods. They were the closest things to wealth in traditional society, but they were more like treasures.

Of all the Hawaiian treasures in the islands, Native Hawaiian scholar Davida Malo wrote, *hulu manu* (feathers) were greatly held in esteem and they were the most prized. They were made into *ʻahu ʻula* (literally "red capes or cloaks"), insignia for battle that were reserved, according to Malo, for true warriors and not for those who were warriors in name only. These *ʻahu ʻula* were for distinguished and high chiefs and not for the lesser chiefs.

There were many forms of *ʻahu ʻula*, ranging from a rectangular to a crescent shape. While red and yellow feathers predominate, brown and black were also used. The capes were decorated with many different designs, which some believe may represent the symbols of the *aliʻi* and the gods: the rainbow, the teeth of sharks or lightning. The size of the cape and the amount of feathers used had a direct relation to the extent of the *aliʻi's* power.

Malo states that the one made only from yellow mamo feathers was reserved for the *aliʻi ʻaimoku*, the paramount chief. Such was the *ʻahu ʻula* of Kamehameha I. It was "made from some 450,000 of the rarest feathers of the mamo, representing by one calculation more than 80,000 birds, since each bird yielded only six or seven suitable feathers," wrote Bishop Museum curator Roger Rose, adding that the "acquisition of this much wealth could have been achieved only by a paramount chief having the sources of supply under his control."

These chiefly treasures were also used as gifts of exchange by the *aliʻi*. Most *ʻahu ʻula* in existence today are to be found outside of the Hawaiian Islands, as they were given away to visiting foreigners. The first example was recorded during Captain James Cook's encounter with Kalaniʻōpuʻu, the paramount chief of the island of Hawaiʻi. According to the journal of one of Cook's men:

"... the King got up & threw in a graceful manner over the Captains Shoulders the Cloak he himself wore, & put a featherd Cap upon his head, & a very handsome fly flap [kāhili] in his hand; besides which he laid down at the Captains feet 5 or 6 Cloaks more, all very beautiful, & to them of the greatest Value ..."

Another example was recorded during the Russian exploration visit of the *Rurick*, captained by Otto von Kotzebue in 1816. When well supplied by Kamehameha, Kotzebue returned the generosity by giving two brass 8-pound mortars, a

PREVIOUS PAGES:

Kamehameha's cape made of approximately 450,000 of the rarest feathers from the mamo bird. Since each bird yielded only six or seven suitable feathers, this may represent as many as 80,000 birds. Bishop Museum, Provisional Government Collection 1893

ABOVE:

Tusk anklet, turtle kūpeʻe (bracelet) said to have been worn by chief of Kauaʻi and brought by ancestors from Tahiti, boar's tooth kūpeʻe. Bishop Museum Collection

keg of wine and some apples from California, and "Upon the expressed wish of Captain von Kotzebue ... Kamehameha had a feather cloak brought out and gave it to Kotzebue for delivery to Emperor Alexander."

There are several traditional accounts of such exchanges. It is said that when Kaumuali'i ceded the island of Kaua'i to Kamehameha in 1810, Kamehameha in return gave him a feather helmet, two feather cloaks and perhaps a feather *malo*.

These were worn by men, but women *ali'i* and other women of authority, as well as men, wore neck and head leis made of the velvety feathers of the native honeycreepers.

So important were these treasures that *ali'i* sought out feathers through tribute and "taxes" or through the exchange of gifts. One chief, Kapohu, sought these treasures from another, Keawehano, the chief of Hilo. When Kapohu was welcomed by Keawehano to come into his home, Kapohu chanted:

From Kahuku to 'Ōla'a I have traveled
To the uplands of Pana'ewa
To the uplands of Haili
To catch the birds with lime,
To catch birds with snares,
To catch birds with lines,
To twist the necks of birds
For their feathers.
Give me a feather cape,
Give me a feather helmet,
Give me a feather necklace.

Other articles made with feathers were *kāhili*, the cylindrical feather standards, which could serve as a sign marking the direction in which the chiefs traveled as well as the location where the chiefs stayed. Smaller hand-held *kāhili* were used to wave over the resting chiefs as a fan and a fly whisk. The feathers of the native goose, owl, the honeycreepers, sea birds like the frigate, and tropic birds were prized to use in *kāhili*.

Another symbol that distinguished the *ali'i nui* (high chief) was the *niho palaoa*, the whale's tooth pendant. It was worn at battle and at less demanding occasions.

Native Hawaiian historian Samuel Mānaiakalani Kamakau wrote that there were two styles of pendants: an *'ōpu'u* (bud) shape, which was worn by the ruling chiefs of O'ahu, and a "tongue-shape hook, like a tortoise-shell fishhook," favored by the chiefs of the island of Hawai'i. These pendants were like national treasures and symbolic of the paramount chief's sovereignty.

Contact with European and American explorers and adventurers brought about the introduction of Western goods, and this had a tremendous influence upon the treasures of the *ali'i*. Davida Malo noted that from the time of Kamehameha I to when Malo was writing during the reign of Kamehameha III, there had been many new introductions, such as clothing, animals, plants and even the concept of wealth. Was the Hawaiians' immense desire of these goods prompted by a recognition of a more advanced technology or a loss of value for traditional things, or the appeal of something new and exotic?

Early accounts of foreigners emphasized the idea that traditional Hawaiian society was under a "cultural fatigue," which could explain why the *kapu* system ended, the destruction

Continued on page 96

ABOVE:

Symbols of royalty that distinguished the ali'i nui (high chief) included feather leis, capes and helmets.

RIGHT:
Model wearing a royal lei niho palaoa. This photo by the author illustrates the ancient custom of bleaching one's hair in the short cropped fashion of the time. Lei niho palaoa courtesy Betty Lou and Don Severson Collection

RIGHT:
King Kalākaua koa calabash bowl stamped with his identifying double "K" marking, feather head lei. Roy Blackshear Collection

Ka'ahumanu, Kamehameha's favorite wife, was proud, regal and admired. She loved beautiful things and took care in keeping herself beautifully dressed. Because of her high rank she had first choice of the best made tapa cloth from all islands. They say that women feared her because she showed favor towards men but this was to change after Ka'ahumanu embraced the word of God.

Ka'ahumanu, wrapped in the finest tapa cloth is holding a hand kāhili, symbol of her rank and status. On her neck is a faceted bead necklace similar to the one pictured. Faceted beads were of European influence and obtained through trading with visiting ships. They were highly prized by 19th century island woman but only the elite among them had access to these treasures.

Ivory and red bead hook pendant necklace, Bishop Museum Collection. Illustration, Hawai'i Historical Society.

III
Lith de Langlumé

FASHION'S QUEEN...

Nāmāhana, one of the widows of Kamehameha I, was acting regent and co-ruler of O'ahu in 1824 when Russian Lt. Otto von Kotzebue came to pay his respects. He noted that "she was exactly six feet 2 inches high and rather more than forty five inches in circumference." Known as the fashion pacesetter of her day, she greeted him in a European dress of lovely blue silk. Kotzebue wrote, "Even among the lowest class of people, some article of European clothing is universal...The females especially set their hearts upon the most fashionable mode of dress: whatever the Queen wears is their model, which they imitate to the utmost of their power." Hawai'i State Archives

Kīna'u, daughter of Kamehameha I, high chiefess and successor as kuhina-niu to Ka'ahumanu. Shown here in a lithograph by J. Masselot, 1837 with her attendants leaving church in their "Sunday best" mu'umu'us. Courtesy of Hawai'i State Archives.

Proud and blissful in their nakedness for centuries, the native population could not comprehend the foreigner's view that a lack of clothing was painful to the eye and injurious to morals. Court fashions in the 1820's was described by one observer in an amusing way, "one of the queen dowagers wearing 72 yards of orange and kersey-mere which was wrapped around her waist until her arms were sustained in a horizontal position ... the remainder formed into a train supported by her attendants."

of religious temples and images, and the general acceptance of Christianity and of Western goods. More recent scholars' interpretations reveal the desire of Western goods, particularly among the *ali'i*, as a continuance of power, rank and status.

Certainly the materials, the usage and durability of Western goods were acknowledged by Hawaiians. Malo wrote,

"There is an abundance of iron now days … it is the new adzes as the stone adze has disappeared from use today, … There are many things considered as wealth today, particularly those things made by hand. But, there are other kinds of wealth today from the foreign lands such as cows, horses, mules, donkeys, goats, sheep as well as the traditional pig, dog and chicken. There are many new birds. Lole, that cloth is the new kapa [bark cloth] as traditional kapa has rapidly disappeared. There are new adzes and there are many new things …"

A good example of this change occurred when the artist Louis Choris set out to paint a portrait of Kamehameha I during the visit of the *Rurick*. Kamehameha greeted the captain and others in front of the thatched houses at Kamakahonu, his home in Kailua-Kona. Dressed in a red *malo* and black *kapa* wrap, he sat upon a raised terrace, on a fine mat, surrounded by his queens and principal chiefs. Choris, who wanted to paint Kamehameha in this black *kapa* wrap, wrote:

"I sought permission … to do his portrait; this proposal seemed to please him, but he suggested that I should step outside a moment as he wished to dress himself; it was not long before he called me back; one may judge at my surprise when I saw the monarch strutting about in a sailor suit; he had on a pair of blue trousers, a red vest, a clean white shirt, and a yellow silk necktie. I begged him to change his costume, but he positively refused, and insisted on being painted as he was dressed."

Choris wanted an image of a native chief and, to his shock, that is not how Kamehameha wanted to be portrayed. Kamehameha wanted to be seen by Europeans as being like them. This doesn't necessarily mean that he was giving up traditional Hawaiian culture; he had greeted the Russian delegation in traditional *ali'i* clothing—a red *malo* and black *kapa*. His choice of his acquired foreign clothing for a portrait, which he understood was to be seen by other Europeans, was, no doubt, his gesture of showing that he was no different from them. Of course, that perception was not shared by Choris.

Not until several years later, after Kamehameha's death, did a fundamental change begin to take place in the *ali'i* attitude toward the function of traditional clothing as a symbol of rank and status. In 1825, Hawaiians made preparations for the return of Kamehameha II and court from their journey to England, not knowing that the king and his wife, Kamāmalu, had died in London. A feather *pā'ū* (skirt), said to be the first and only one of its kind, had been made for Kamehameha II's younger sister, Nāhi'ena'ena, to wear. American missionaries had exerted their influence on the princess, and missionary Charles Stewart wrote of the feather *pā'ū*:

"It was the desire of the chiefs that she should wear it, with the wreaths for the head and neck, necessary to form the complete ancient costume of a princess at this interview; but as it was necessary, in order to do

Continued on page 107

The finest tapa cloth was reserved for the high ranking chiefs. ʻIeʻie baskets stained with kukui.

Yellow and black ʻōʻō and red ʻiʻiwi feathers. This feather cape was given to the queen by her mother, Keohokalole. Bishop Museum Collection. A Boston news reporter wrote of Queen Liliʻuokalani's rare ʻōʻō feather cape, "...Other kingdoms have their costly jewels and brilliant regalia, but for a royal mantle there is probably not one that could compare in elegance with this [that]...its worth is equal to that of any royal robe in existence is quite credible."

Boston Morning Journal, December 28, 1896.

RIGHT:

Liliʻuokalani feather cape.

ABOVE:
Kalākaua Ring of State.
Etruscan gold with carnelian engraved intaglio Hawaiian coat of arms. Two Hawaiian chiefs are carved in full relief, to the side of each is a solitaire one carat diamond. Bishop Museum Collection

There was a renewed interest in the ancient traditions during Kalākaua's reign. The Board of Genealogy of Hawaiian Chiefs was organized in 1882. The King was interested in uncovering the secret of Kamehameha's burial site. When he found what he believed to be the bones of the great king he wrapped them together with his coronation Ring of State and deposited them in the Royal Mausoleum on the night of Kāne, February 8, 1888. It was later learned that the bones were not of Kamehameha and the historic ring was given to the Bishop Museum to ensure proper care.

Kapi'olani's compact, Bernice Pauahi Bishop's marble box. Bishop Museum Collection

KULIA • I • KANUU

RIGHT:
Queen Kapi'olani's famed peacock gown, designed for her to wear at Queen Victoria's Jubilee, created a fashion sensation. Princess Lili'uokalani (woman on left) was the Queen's traveling companion, and served as an interpreter since Kapi'olani did not speak English.
Hawai'i State Archives

LEFT:
Queen Emma in a typical European style gown which inspired the design of the formal version of the Hawaiian mu'umu'u, the holokū with its long flowing train. Photo, Hawai'i State Archives

ABOVE:
A rare image of the royal family. From left: Queen Kalama, Alexander Liholiho, King Kamehameha III, Lot Kamehameha, and Victoria Kamāmalu. In the foreground, a kukui nut necklace that belonged to Bernice Pauahi Bishop. Courtesy: Kamehameha Schools/ Bernice Pauahi Bishop Estate

ABOVE:

A group of nobles and two future kings. Circa 1872. Third from left, King Lunalilo; far right, King Kalākaua.

Photo: Bishop Museum Archives

this, that she should be naked to the waist, nothing could induce her to consent. To escape importunity, she fled to the Mission House early in the morning. She wept so as scarcely to be pacified by us, and returned to the chiefs only in time to take her seat, and have it thrown carelessly about her over her European dress ..."

Although she did wear the feather *pā'ū* later at other ceremonial occasions, this event marked a changing attitude toward the function of feather garments, and signaled an end to the making of them. Feathers could still be used for taxes to the kingdom as late as the 1860s, but the massive destruction of birds and their habitat also contributed to the discontinuance of this treasure.

The succeeding royalty until the time of the Kalākaua dynasty showed very little association with these traditional treasures. Their choice of dress was European or military and the adornment was modern: medals, rings, necklaces, earrings and bracelets. The symbol of state became a military sword. During Kalākaua's reign, a new palace was built and other European symbols of state were introduced, such as a royal scepter, ring of state, crowns and thrones.

Traditional treasures took on a new function as each royal family amassed inherited or collected artifacts. Photographs of these collections show them massively displayed as if making a statement about the families' "wealth" of traditional treasures to be equated to a sense of higher rank of genealogical and chiefly status linked with the past.

When the estate of C. Kana'ina, King Lunalilo's father, was put to auction, it was one of the first attempts to place a monetary value upon traditional treasures. Many of the items of that estate were purchased for the kingdom's new National Museum.

The museum was established by the Legislature to display the Kingdom's national treasures for public viewing, particularly for the increasing number of overseas visitors. Set up in a corner of the second floor of Ali'iōlani Hale, the National Museum was opened to the public on November 8, 1875. Its collections were gathered from an exhibit that had been sent to Paris and various donations and acquisitions from private collections including the Kana'ina estate.

An attempt to revitalize traditional practices during Kalākaua's reign was his founding of the Hale Nauā Society for the "revival of Ancient Science of Hawai'i in combination with the promotion and advancement of Modern Sciences, Art, Literature, and Philanthropy." Members used the *niho palaoa*, "feather" cloaks, and other traditional things for "Masonic-like ritual," but the materials they were made of were not the same as before, as rare or extinct birds' feathers and whales' teeth gave way to the use of crepe paper and walrus ivory.

The Kalākaua dynasty reinforced this commitment to revival by having official photographic portraits taken with feather cloaks draped upon the royal thrones in the background. This also revealed the change in attitudes toward traditional treasures, now artifacts, for the monarchs were never again pictured wearing these insignia of rank, status and sovereignty of their ancestors.

HĀNAI SISTERS

There is no word in the English language for "hānai", the Hawaiian custom of giving your precious child to another to raise as their own. The act of doing this helped fortify friendship and loyalty among the chiefly families. Later this practice was followed by the commoners. Bernice Pauahi and Lydia Kamaka'eha were hānai sisters. Lydia was given to Bernice's parents, high chief Pākī and his wife Kōnia, soon after birth. They were educated at the missionary Chiefs Children's School, making their mark in later years as two of the most loved and highly regarded women in Hawai'i's history. Bernice refused the throne twice but dedicated her life to good works. Lydia ascended to the throne after her brother King Kalākaua died and took the name, Lili'uokalani.

Photo: Kamehameha Schools/Bernice Pauahi Bishop Estate Archives

ABOVE:

The "aloha bracelet" was a loving gift from Bernice to Lili'uokalani made of the braided hair of their father Pākī. Bishop Museum Collection

...Whilst humbly meditating
Within these walls imprisoned
Thou art my light my haven
Thy glory my support.

Look not on their failings
Nor the sins of men
Forgive with loving kindness
That we might be made pure.

For thy grace I beseech thee
Bring us neath thy protection
Now and forever more. Amen.

"Queen's Prayer."
Written by Queen Lili'uokalani in March 1895 while imprisoned at 'Iolani Palace and dedicated to her niece Victoria Ka'iulani. Ka'iulani photo: Hawai'i State Archives

Victoria Kaiulani

Queen Victoria of England consented to be the godmother to "Little Prince" Albert. In commemoration of the baptismal, she sent his parents Queen Emma and Kamehameha IV a sterling silver Christening cup. Unfortunately, the cup arrived only days before the prince died of what was thought to be brain fever. The grief of the nation over his death was immeasurable.

Silver christening cup photo: Bishop Museum Archives.

Prince Albert's christening gown and crib, Queen Emma Summer Palace, courtesy of Daughters of Hawai'i.

By the 1880's court fashion was decidedly European. Hawai'i's ladies did their best to keep up with the latest trends.

LEFT:
Coronation gown.
RIGHT:
Bernice Pauahi dress. Both reproductions from the Richard Goodwin Collection, courtesy of Ray Sasaki, Jr.

117 & 118, Leadenhall Street

London, E.C. Nov. 20th 1882

Mr Col. C. H. Judd

Coronation a/c.

In account with A. Hoffnung & Co.

		£	s	d	
To	2 Richly Jewelled Crowns manufactured throughout of solid Gold (15 & 18 carats fine) & studded entirely with real Gems consisting of Diamonds (brilliants & roses) Opals Emeralds Rubies & Pearls.	1000	"	"	
"	2 Silk Velvet linings for the above	3	12	.	
"	1 Emboyna Wood Case " " " lined with white Satin, brass handles lock & key	10	10	"	
"	1 Solid fine Gold Coronation Ring having in Centre a Red Onyx Stone upon which is engraved the Hawaiian Arms - the bearers & crown chased up in Solid Gold & set with 2 Brilliants	25	"	"	
"	1 Solid Leather Outside case for Crowns &c.	3	"	"	
"	1 Sceptre to Special Order made of fine Silver & richly gilt with Pure Gold	12	12		
"	Preparing drawing & design for above	1	5	.	1055 19 .
		1055	19		
"	2000 Invitation Cards printed in 5 Colors in English, Crest of Arms &c @ 16/8 p 100.	16	13	4	
"	2000 Ditto in Hawaiian " 16/8 " "	16	13	4	
"	3000 ditto Crown & Cushion printed				

PONI MŌʻĪ

the Coronation

CHAPTER THREE

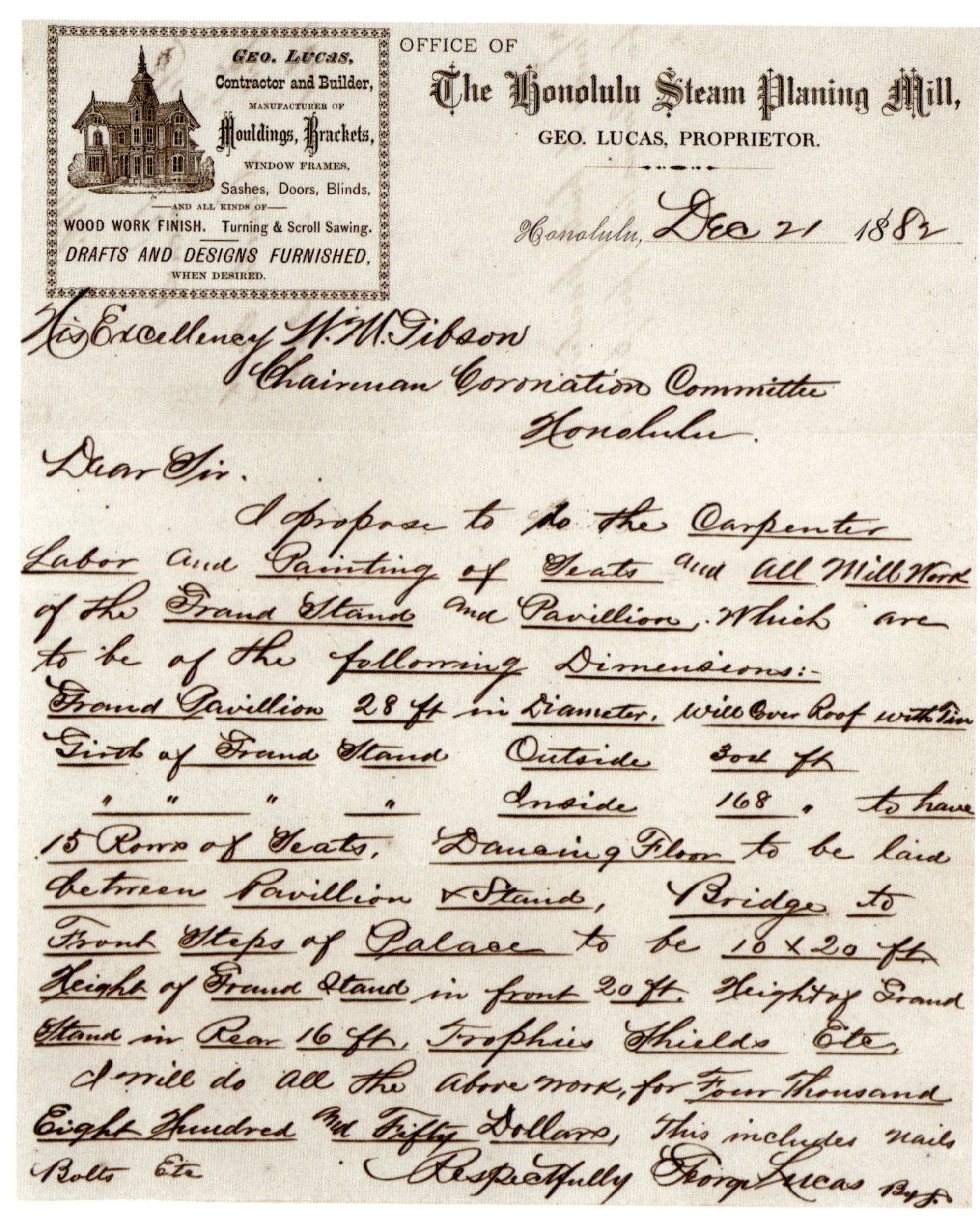

GEO. LUCAS,
Contractor and Builder,
MANUFACTURER OF
Mouldings, Brackets,
WINDOW FRAMES,
Sashes, Doors, Blinds,
—AND ALL KINDS OF—
WOOD WORK FINISH. Turning & Scroll Sawing.
DRAFTS AND DESIGNS FURNISHED,
WHEN DESIRED.

OFFICE OF
The Honolulu Steam Planing Mill,
GEO. LUCAS, PROPRIETOR.

Honolulu, Dec 21 1882

His Excellency W. M. Gibson
Chairman Coronation Committee
Honolulu.

Dear Sir.

I propose to do the Carpenter Labor and Painting of Seats and All Mill Work of the Grand Stand and Pavillion, Which are to be of the following Dimensions:-
Grand Pavillion 28 ft in Diameter, Will Cover Roof with Tin
Girth of Grand Stand Outside 300 ft
" " " " Inside 168 " to have
15 Rows of Seats, Dancing Floor to be laid between Pavillion & Stand, Bridge to Front Steps of Palace to be 10 x 20 ft
Height of Grand Stand in front 20 ft. Height of Grand Stand in Rear 16 ft, Trophies Shields Etc,
I will do All the above work, for Four Thousand Eight Hundred and Fifty Dollars, This includes nails Bolts Etc

Respectfully George Lucas

ABOVE:

Architectural plans for Kalākaua coronation stand.

Hawai'i State Archives

King Kalākaua did not have a formal coronation until the ninth anniversary of his inauguration ...and then he planned the most grand event of all. A coronation stand was built with a bridge connecting it to the palace's first floor veranda. The amphitheater around it could seat several thousand spectators. The lavish event put a strain on the kingdom's budget. While some were quick to mock and criticize, others found it to be a source of inspiration and pride. The local paper reported, "...brilliant weather continued and strange to say, but nevertheless true, a star was seen in the heavens at 8:00 AM shining contemporaneously with the sun. The Hawaiians regard this as a happy omen. Other remarkable freaks of nature were observable to all. At 11:00 AM the sun was obscured by clouds, and remained so until the very moment of 'Crowning' was being solemnized. Like the mechanical transformation scene to take place at an appointed minute, so did the sun burst forth as the clock struck twelve and immediately after their majesties had been crowned."

ABOVE:

Coronation invitation.

Roy Blackshear Collection

When David Kalākaua was elected king by the Legislature in 1874, it was in a stormy election battle with Queen Emma, followed by rioting by her supporters. The new king was hastily inaugurated the next day with a minimum of ceremony.

Nine years later, having traveled around the world and observed the grandeur, pomp and ceremony of monarchies elsewhere, Kalākaua was inspired to hold an elaborate formal coronation at his newly completed ʻIolani Palace. Befitting his kingly dignity, it would compensate for his unceremonious earlier inauguration.

The date chosen for the coronation was February 12, 1883, the ninth anniversary of his accession to the throne.

Crowns for King Kalākaua and Queen Kapiʻolani, a sword of state, a royal scepter and ring of state were ordered from England.

For the ceremony, an octagonal Coronation Pavilion was built in front of the palace. (Afterwards it was moved to its present site on the palace grounds.) Around it a temporary amphitheater was erected to seat several thousand spectators.

From all parts of the islands, crowds thronged to Honolulu for the coronation and the two week celebration that followed.

On the chosen morning, a fanfare of trumpets at about eleven o'clock heralded the procession of the royal family, attended by numerous *kāhili* bearers, from the palace into the Coronation Pavilion. Kalākaua was resplendent in a white uniform with the decorations of many royal orders gleaming on his chest. Queen Kapiʻolani was regally garbed in gold embroidered white satin and crimson velvet with a long train trimmed with ermine.

Though fond of European style pomp and ceremony, Kalākaua also had a deep appreciation of Hawaiian traditions. At his coronation, he was invested with symbols of sovereignty that were a mixture of European royal regalia and ancient Hawaiian emblems of exalted rank.

Princess Poʻomaikelani, sister of the queen, presented the king with the *pūloʻuloʻu*, the kapu stick, and the *niho palaoa*, the whale' s tooth pendant traditionally worn by high chiefs.

Most prized of the ancient Hawaiian royal symbols was the great yellow feather cloak of Kamehameha I, outshining in its beauty and rarity all the modern monarchial ornaments. Princess Kekaulike, the queen' s youngest sister, gave the cloak to the chancellor, who draped it over the king' s shoulders, with the words, "Receive this ancient royal mantle of your predecessors as the ensign of knowledge and wisdom."

The chancellor presented Kalākaua with the sword of state, the ring of state and the royal scepter.

Prince Kawānanakoa, the king and queen's nephew, came forward with the crowns. The chancellor placed the king's crown before him, saying, "Receive this crown of pure gold to adorn the high station wherein thou has been placed." Robed in the magnificent feather cloak of Kamehameha, King Kalākaua lifted the jeweled crown and placed it on his own head. The king then crowned his queen, saying, "I place this crown upon your head, to she the honors of my throne."

Following a prayer, the shore batteries and the foreign warships in the harbor fired a salute, and the choir burst forth with an anthem composed for the occasion, "Cry Out Isles with Joy!" The king and queen led the procession into the palace as the Royal Hawaiian Band played the "Coronation March."

The telephone and electric lights came to the 'Iolani Palace. Then, in 1888, the tracks for tramcars were put in place. The Hawai'i Tramways Company, Ltd., was authorized to use electric traction in 1890 but horse and mule was still favored. Here we see the King Street line with the Opera House to the right and Ali'iōlani Hale (Government Office Building) on the left.
Photo: Hawai'i State Archives

RIGHT:

'Iolani Palace circa 1885.

ABOVE:

Palace dance card and gold embossed Hawai'i coat of arms from 'Iolani Palace stationery.

The ceremony ended, the celebration began. The festivities included a coronation ball, fireworks displays, a state dinner, a regatta, horse races, a giant lūʻau attended by some 5,000 guests, and hula performances each night on the palace grounds.

Supporters of the monarchy thought the coronation impressive and appropriate, and they enjoyed the festivities. The Native Hawaiians especially loved the hula performances, since for decades the dance had rarely been seen in public, a victim of missionary zealotry.

The king's detractors, particularly residents of foreign blood in the business community, considered the coronation and celebration a wanton waste of money.

The king's sister, Liliʻuokalani, defended the coronation as serving "a serious purpose of national importance," confirming the ascendancy of the Kalākaua line as the ruling dynasty of Hawaiʻi.

Liliʻuokalani wrote, "Certainly the coronation celebration had been a great success. The people from the country and from the other islands went back to their homes with a renewed sense of dignity and honor involved in their nationality, and an added interest in the administration of their government."

She declared, "It was wise and patriotic to spend money to awaken in the people a national pride."

The opposition newspapers voiced bitter criticism. *Planters' Monthly* attacked the coronation's "follies and extravagances," and denounced the hula performances as "a retrograde step of heathenism and a disgrace to the age." The *Hawaiian Gazette* ranted that the hulas were "the very apotheosis of grossness."

Some hulas honoring Kalākaua had been specially composed for the celebration. At one such performance, a local attorney, William R. Castle, son of a missionary-turned-businessman, asked for a translation of the Hawaiian words on the printed hula program. Shocked, he brought obscenity charges against one of the king' s aides and the printer of the program. At the hearing, witnesses pointed out that in ancient Hawaiian tradition certain kinds of chants have always honored various parts of the human body, including the procreative parts of the king or chief. Nonetheless, the defendants were fined.

Kalākaua continued vigorously to lead a revival of hula and other Hawaiian cultural traditions. His enduring legacy to his people was a sense of pride in their Hawaiian heritage.

The crowns of King Kalākaua and Queen Kapiʻolani, identical except in size, are of velvet and solid gold set with precious gems. Though fashioned in the European monarchial style, they have a distinctly Hawaiian motif: taro leaves. The border of golden taro leaves is highlighted with four Maltese crosses. Together, they represent the blending of Hawaiian and European cultural elements, for which Kalākaua's reign was known.

From the center of the cross in the front of each crown glows a magnificent six carat diamond. The golden band that forms the crown's base is richly bejeweled with diamonds, opals, emeralds and rubies and, in the back, six highly polished reddish-black kukui nuts.

Rising from the gold band and extending over the crimson velvet cap are eight bars of gold, symbolizing the eight major Hawaiian Islands united under one rule. The eight golden bars unite at the top of the crown, supporting a dark red enamel

Continued on page 135

LEFT:

"Dandy" Ioane 'Ūkēkē with his hula dancers, 1886-1891. King Kalākaua revived the ancient art of hula with the help of colorful hula master Ioane 'Ūkēkē who gave command performances for the royal court. Photo: Hawai'i State Archives

The Imperial German Government sent Captain Henry Berger (pictured on page 129) to Hawai'i when King Kamehameha V requested a skilled bandmaster to organize the Royal Hawaiian Band. Berger took the small group of inexperienced musicians, many of them taken from the Honolulu Boy's Reform School, and turned them into a world renowned band. No doubt, his experience as the German army bandmaster helped. He ruled his band like a king with an iron fist and remained in command for 43 years.

FOLLOWING PAGES:

Left page: Henry Berger's pocket watch, photo of Berger with his wife Rose, gold pin from Royal Hawaiian Band, his Elks Club pin, gold tipped baton inscribed with respect from the band members, uniform buttons. Right page: Berger's medals and gold medallion from Queen Kapi'olani, February 12, 1879. All courtesy of Rose M. Berger Trust, Edward Stanley, trustee. Musical programme and Palace menu, courtesy Donald H. Graham Jr. Collection.

GRAVELOTTE-ST. PRIVAT
SEDAN
PARIS
MUSICAL PROGRAMME
GIVEN BY THE
ROYAL HAWAIIAN MILITARY BAND.
On Friday morning
Birthday
March United States Berger
Overture America Catlin
Finale Bivouac Petrella
Waltz Jubilant Fahrbach
Polka Amager Godfrey
Medley Pleasant Memories Beyer
Star Spangled Banner
Hawaii Ponoi
Febr. 22. 1889.
Honolulu, H.I.
H. Berger, Band Master

21 JEWELS
H Berger.
Bandmaster Haw. Band
Honolulu. H. Isl.

Queen Kapiʻolani

The Mayor of Boston
requests the pleasure of your company
to meet
Her Majesty Queen Kapiolani
and Her Royal Highness
The Princess Liliuokalani
of the Hawaiian Islands
at the Mechanics'
on Thursday
at Eight
City Hall, May 1887.
The Lord Chamberlain is
commanded by The Queen to invite
H. E. Lt. General Dominis
to an Afternoon Party on Wednesday the
29th of June 1887 from 5 to 7 o'Clock.
Buckingham Palace
Morning Dress

ABOVE:

Inspired by Queen Victoria's Golden Jubilee in England, Lili'uokalani composed a song to express her feelings. Had she not been remembered as Hawai'i's queen, Lili'uokalani would still be treasured by her people as a masterful musician.

Floyd Ho'opi'i Collection

RIGHT:
A brooch of diamonds, rubies and pearl was a gift to Kapiʻolani from the Prince of Wales (later King Edward VII). It was attached to a small bouquet of flowers and given to her to commemorate Queen Victoria's Golden Jubilee.
Bishop Museum Collection

ABOVE:

Royal Order of Kapi'olani Officer Cross created by Kalākaua in 1880 to honor Kapi'olani the Great, his Queen's namesake. It was awarded for excellence in the arts, sciences, charity, and service to the Kingdom. The medallion reads, "Kūlia i ka nu'u", or "strive for the summit," which was Queen Kapi'olani's motto. Don Medcalf Collection

Your Sister and Cousin Victoria R.I.

Kapi'olani's diamond and ruby butterfly brooch and gold compact with the Crest of Kapi'olani presented by Queen Victoria at 1887 Jubilee. Bishop Museum Collection

globe banded with pearls and surmounted by a diamond studded Maltese cross. Each crown contains 521 diamonds, 54 pearls, 20 opals, eight emeralds, eight rubies, one garnet and six polished *kukui* nuts.

In 1893, following the overthrow of the Hawaiian monarchy, the jewels were stolen from King Kalākaua's crown at 'Iolani Palace.

The mystery surrounding the theft of the crown jewels at first baffled the police. The case was placed in the hands of officer William Larsen, who expressed his dismay at the lack of clues. After many weeks of work, he had a suspect: a young American named George Ryan, who had enlisted as a soldier in the regular forces of the new provisional government and had been on guard duty at the palace in early April when the jewels were stolen. Larsen learned that he had sold an unmounted diamond to an acquaintance and, on June 13th, searching Ryan's room, he discovered a dozen diamonds wrapped in tissue paper. Arrested that night, Ryan was charged with larceny of the crown jewels. In late July, he escaped by scaling the wall of O'ahu Jail. He was later recaptured, tried and convicted. Six more of the 361 diamonds stolen from the crown were recovered from the home of Ryan's sister in Arkansas.

The vandalized crown was all but forgotten for many years, until 1925 when the Legislature appropriated funds for its restoration. The royal Hawaiian crowns resided at Bishop Museum until 1990, when they were transferred to 'Iolani Palace in a ceremony on November 16, King Kalākaua's birthday. The crowns, accompanied by the royal scepter and sword of state, were formally received at the palace by Abigail Kekaulike

Kawānanakoa, a descendant of the royal family.

Throughout the period of the Hawaiian monarchy, the islands' rulers had maintained close ties with Britain, ties that had been strengthened by King Kalākaua's visit there on his world tour in 1881. With gladness the Hawaiian royal family accepted the invitation to the great celebration in London commemorating Queen Victoria's Golden Jubilee, June 20th, 1887, the 50th anniversary of her accession to the throne of Great Britain.

Queen Kapi'olani headed the Hawai'i delegation to the Jubilee. Accompanying her were Crown Princess Lili'uokalani, her husband, General John O. Dominis, and other members of the court. The king appointed his chamberlain, Colonel Curtis Pi'ehu I'aukea, to serve as translator for Queen Kapi'olani, who did not speak English.

Sailing from Honolulu April 12th, the royal party spent some time in the United States before going to England. In Washington, the queen and princess were warmly received and entertained by President Grover Cleveland and the first lady, who hosted an elegant formal dinner at the White House in their honor. (Six years later, when the Hawaiian monarchy was overthrown during Lili'uokalani's reign, this same American president would vigorously advocate her restoration to the throne.) After visiting Boston and New York, the royal party sailed for England.

Arriving in Liverpool, the Hawaiian queen and princess received a grand welcome from officials, including the lord mayor. They were also met by a splendid military escort of about 100 soldiers, specially detailed by Queen Victoria to do the visitors honor.

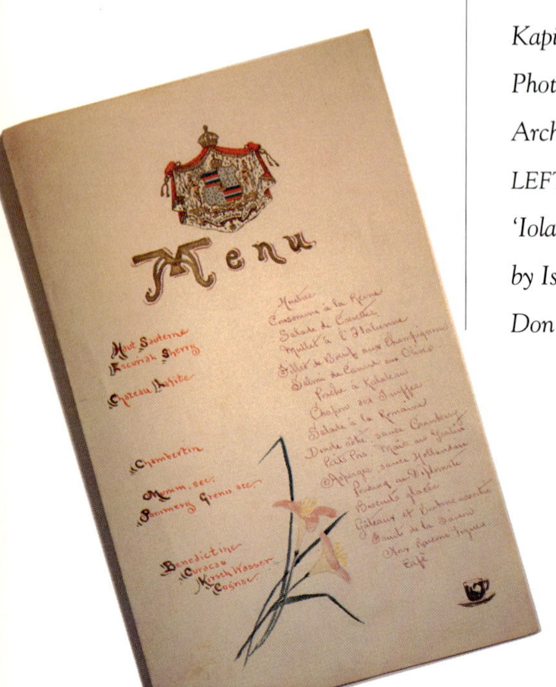

ABOVE:

Kapi'olani Coronation crown. Photo: Bishop Museum Photo Archives

LEFT:

'Iolani Palace hand painted menu by Isabell Strong, Don Medcalf Collection.

In London, Queen Victoria received Queen Kapiʻolani, Princess Liliʻuokalani and Colonel Iʻaukea in private audience at Buckingham Palace. The British queen greeted the Hawaiian queen and princess with a kiss, received Queen Kapiʻolani's congratulations, and thanked her for coming so far to see her. She spoke with enthusiasm of her earlier pleasure in meeting King Kalākaua, saying she had never forgotten his agreeable visit.

The following day was the main ceremony of Queen Victoria's Jubilee, a service of thanksgiving at historic Westminster Abbey, where she had been crowned 50 years earlier. It was a day of pageantry, tradition and rejoicing.

The streets through which the caravan of carriages passed on its way to the Abbey were elaborately decorated with flags and streamers and thronged with people who greeted their queen, and each carriage bearing her distinguished guests, with resounding cheers.

At the Abbey, Queen Kapiʻolani and Princess Liliʻuokalani were seated on a raised platform surrounded by kings and queens, princes and princesses from around the world. Flourishes of trumpets announced the entrance of the British royal family. To the stately strains of "God Save the Queen," the 68-year-old monarch, attired in a black gown and diamond jewelry, ascended the dais in the center of the great church and seated herself in the coronation chair.

The ceremonial service, led by the archbishop of Canterbury, was impressive. At its conclusion, Queen Victoria received the homage of her children and grandchildren, kissing each in turn, and they responded with a kiss on her royal hand.

Following the service, at the Jubilee banquet held for visiting royalty at Buckingham Palace, Queen Kapiʻolani was escorted by the Price of Wales, and Princess Liliʻuokalani by the Duke of Edinburgh, another of Queen Victoria's sons.

After the banquet, the British monarch led the royal guests into a side room where the gifts sent in recognition of her Jubilee year were on display. Hawaii's unique gift was a piece of featherwork, using the rare royal feathers to form the monogram "V.R." set in a diamond studded frame.

At the Jubilee, Queen Kapiʻolani wore a special gown of blue velvet lavishly adorned with peacock feathers. It created a sensation in London. The tale behind the gown is that the court designer in Hawaiʻi ran out of peacock feathers from the king's birds before he could complete it. Resourcefully, he spread the rumor among the Hawaiians that keeping peacock feathers in the home brought bad luck. He soon had enough feathers to finish the gown.

The Jubilee celebration continued with a grand ball and many other brilliant social events. The Hawaiian queen and princess gained a lasting impression of the friendly feeling of the British royal family and the English people for them and the kingdom of Hawaiʻi.

Queen Kapiʻolani and her party had planned to tour the continent, but they received the alarming news of a revolutionary movement in Hawaiʻi, directed against the monarchy by men of foreign blood, who had forced the king to sign the Bayonet Constitution. With apprehension they departed at once for Hawaiʻi.

Arriving in Honolulu July 26th, the queen and princess were royally welcomed by a friendly crowd, as usual. But, it was a troubled kingdom to which they returned with their cherished memories of Queen Victoria's Jubilee.

HO‘OILINA

the Legacy

CHAPTER FOUR

During the reign of Kamehameha III, there developed an awareness of the rights of the *kānaka*, the people or commoners. Their labor had been abused during the massive effort to harvest sandalwood for the chiefs, and their oppression was furthered when property ownership resulted from the Great Mahele of 1848, that is the division of lands between the king, the government and the chiefs. Citizens felt themselves being disenfranchised by the growing influence and land ownership of foreigners, who bought land from the chiefs, and a protest broke out in the late 1840s on the island of Maui. It bordered on near rebellion. These concerns led to the establishment of the Kuleana Lands, an additional land division for the commoners.

Each dynasty thereafter promoted its concern for the health, welfare and education of the Native Hawaiians, and in particular there was always an apprehension for the declining native population. There were many joint efforts to encourage individual and religious groups to assist these efforts, and the monarchy also engaged in its own private efforts.

King Kamehameha IV and Queen Emma founded a hospital to take care of Native Hawaiians and foreigners who could not afford private care. They also promoted education by the establishment of parochial boys' and girls' schools. Queen Emma's estate and trust later would support the operations of the Queen's Hospital, named in her honor.

King Kalākaua's wife, Queen Kapi'olani, established a maternity hospital, the Queen Kapi'olani Hospital, to "save and preserve the race." King Lunalilo's estate and trust established the Lunalilo Home, to serve and house indigent elderly Hawaiians.

The vast land holdings of the Kamehamehas, which had passed on to the last two of Kamehameha I's grandchildren, Princesses Ruth Ke'elikōlani and Bernice Pauahi, became the resource establishing the Kamehameha Schools. In a very detailed will, Princess Bernice Pauahi Bishop had included a paragraph stating her desire for the establishment of a boys' and a girls' school for Native Hawaiian children. Her husband, Charles Reed Bishop, a successful banker, founded a private museum, the Bernice Pauahi Bishop Museum, to house the vast treasures of the Kamehameha family.

The land holdings of Hawaii'i's last dynasty, in accord with the will of Queen Lili'uokalani, became the trust to serve orphaned and destitute children, with the emphasis on Native Hawaiian children, and built an interisland agency known as the Queen Lili'uokalani Children's Center.

These are the physical and living legacies of Hawai'i's royal dynasties. The land-based estates and trusts have served countless thousands of Native Hawaiians since they were established to save, educate, preserve and perpetuate the Hawaiian race.

Another legacy was made manifest in the founding of the kingdom. This legacy is about Hawaiian leadership, its relationship of rights, privileges and responsibility to the people.

There is a quote attributed to Kamehameha I when he was near death. There are some variants to it, but one version widely used today is: "*E 'oni wale no 'oukou i ko'u pono, 'a'ole e pau*" (Try as you may to undo the good that I have done, you cannot do so). What did he mean by this parting statement which sounds more like a *ho'opāpā*, a taunt or a boast which warriors recited before engaging in combat? The key word he used is *pono* (good), for he indicates *pono* to be what he considered his legacy.

ABOVE, and previous pages:
Children at ʻIolani Palace wall.
Photo: Hawaiʻi State Archives.
RIGHT:
Avenue of Palms, entrance to
Queen's Hospital

Pono is not an easy word to define in precise terms. Davida Malo gives some insights into *pono* and its opposite, *hewa*, describing these words in terms of appropriate behavior and morals.

He wrote that for the ruling *ali'i nui* to be *pono* it was essential that "he had to mālama, protect and take care of, his own people, because they were the true body of the government." Malo stated that "if the people knew the faults of a certain *ali'i* were truly bad, the people also knew of the *pono* of other *ali'i* who were truly good. The *ali'i* who was lethargic, as was the *ali'i* who like to indulge in pleasures, or quarrels, criticizing, envious, greedy, and selfish was to be condemned. The *ali'i* who was reasonable, courteous, tolerant or slow to anger, unpretentious, patient was the *ali'i* who was greatly desired by the people and beloved. The *ali'i* who abused his rule was not well loved by those of his chiefdom, but the *ali'i* who was *pono* to his chiefdom was one who was forever beloved. The *ali'i* who was *pono* to his rule was likened to a powerful being because of his genuine *pono* while the *ali'i* who spoke ill of other *ali'i* was considered *hewa* because of the actual *hewa* that came from his mouth."

Of all the many kinds of *ali'i*, Malo wrote, "There were a few *ali'i* who ruled in *pono* like Kamehameha I who was an *ali'i* that kept the peace (*ho'omalu pono*)."

Samuel Mānaiakalani Kamakau assessed what Kamehameha had done to cause him to taunt anyone to undo what he had done. Kamakau listed many things that Kamehameha did to consolidate the kingdom and to ensure that his rule met the standards of being *pono*.

He wrote that Kamehameha "took care" of the *ali'i* who aided him "to secure his rule, making them administrators in his governance and by giving them large tracts of land."

He established a "deliberative council consisting of his counselors and chiefs selected for the purpose" and there was also a member who was a *kahuna* and an orator. "Kamehameha listened to the advice of others," commented Kamakau. "He was a patient chief and did not instantly avenge an injury, and with compassion for his enemies."

He "made laws to protect both chiefs and commoners, prohibiting murder, theft, wanton destruction, the taking of property without cause, robbing the weak, praying to death, and laws to observe the tabus of the gods." He built *heiau* (temples) and "loved pious people." He proclaimed a law known as Māmalahoe which literally meant "splintered paddle" and protected all people from harm while traveling.

He regulated fishing and fishermen. Kamehameha himself took "part in the work, no matter what kind it was." He selected and encouraged craftsmen to become more productive in the many arts. He "took care of the children of commoners and trained them to be warriors or to learn other arts, and he selected men to act as teachers in the arts." He chose strong paddlers, master navigators and runners to ensure proper communication throughout the islands. "He appointed commoners to the different land divisions to cultivate" (the land). Kamehameha elevated the importance of the annual tribute *(makahiki)* "as a time of rest from labor when men might regain their strength."

To insure his reign from internal threats he "often summoned the chiefs to come and live with him and he discouraged their living far away in the back country where they might gather men...and some day take it [to] conspire against his rule."

He "respected his wives and gave them wealth and honor."

Furthermore, "Kamehameha was known as a good provider, because he supplied the wants of the chiefs high and low, of those who lived with him, and of those who had no master. He did this in order that the people might speak of his kindness and of the pains he took to care for the chiefs and people; the orators were instructed to speak of his kind acts."

Kamakau, like Malo, commented that all of this would "mark the era of peace begun by the rule of Kamehameha over the whole group from Hawai'i to O'ahu." Kamakau's words indicate what Kamehameha had done was a conscientious effort to establish a model or standard for leadership; of what the relationship between Native Hawaiian leaders and the people should be like.

Indeed the actions of Kamehameha were to be lionized not only by his descendants, but also embraced as a form of traditional continuity and identity by the Kalākaua dynasty.

During the reign of King Kalākaua, the 1878 Legislature passed a resolution to construct and erect a statue of Kamehameha I. Kalākaua took a personal interest in this project, advising on the arrangement of the statue's garments and even making a sketch of the spear point for the sculptor.

Four bronze plaques on the pedestal depicted events in the life of Kamehameha I: Kamehameha I aboard Captain James Cook's ship; the warrior-king warding off spears in a traditional rite; the conqueror of islands at Kohala, his home district on the island of Hawai'i; and a scene depicting the Māmalahoe Kanawai, Kamehameha I's famous "law of the splintered paddle," which guaranteed the safety of the pathways and trails to all.

King Kalākaua unveiled the statue on February 14, 1883, as a royal battery fired a salute and the Royal Hawaiian Band played "Hawai'i Pono'ī." This was the new national anthem with words written by Kalākaua, also proclaiming in its refrain: "Makua lani e, Kamehameha, e, Nā kāua e pale, me ka ihe" (Chiefly Father, Kamehameha, By fighting to protect, With spear).

Not everyone was pleased by the erection of this statue. It was reported in newspaper accounts that "some foreign residents had a contemptuous attitude toward the Kamehameha statue and toward other expressions of Hawaiian nationalism."

By immortalizing Kamehameha to mythical proportions we have also idealized his standards of leadership and conduct, his *pono,* as the measure of leadership in the Native Hawaiian community. Where once the names of KalaunuioHua and 'Umi were told in epic and heroic stories, it is now that of Kamehameha.

Unlike *ali'i* before him, Kamehameha forged a new way of governance that might meet the challenges enabling his people to survive in a greater world, but one based in continuity with traditions. The success of that formulation has challenged each generation since his time to uphold or surpass it, until there comes another who will remake it in a way never done before. Until that time his *pono* endures.

Perhaps during a night that is very rainy, when there is thunder and lightning, in what the people of old called 'Ikuwā, the season of the roaring surf, thunder and cloudbursts, the din and voices of the gods in the elements, another child will be born to the hushed whispers of, "Is this the one? Is this the next Kamehameha?"

The Siphon.
1. Which have you here, a state of rest or a state of
2. What forces are acting
3. Which
unequal.
5. When
water stop flowing.
6.
stop flowing then.

Queen Lili'uokalani had a soft spot in her heart for Hawai'i's children and took an active interest in their advancement and well being. A story is told of a June day in 1892 when the Queen and her ladies paid a surprise visit to Kamehameha School for Boys and chanced upon Mr. Uldrick Thompson's lesson on making a cup of coffee. It served as a lesson in etiquette which, it seems, the boys already knew well. Mr. Thompson filled one of the coffee cups and presented it to the Queen, then one for each of the ladies. The Queen sipped it with her compliments. After her departure a cup was poured for each boy but in a gentlemanly tribute they declined. The coffee, they said, was not for them, it was for the Queen. Photo of Mr. Uldrick Thompson and his students, Kamehameha Schools/ Bernice Pauahi Bishop Estate Archives

The signature of Lydia ʻAholo is the first entry in the register of the first class of Kamehameha School for Girls. She lists her address as Washington Place, the Queen's residence. In an interview in 1972, Lydia was 94 but her memory of the Queen was vivid. She was, at that time, the sole survivor of the first graduating class of Kamehameha School for Girls. Soon after Lydia was born on February 6, 1878, in Lahaina, Maui, Liliʻuokalani sent for the baby and her grandparents and installed them in her Honolulu home, Washington Place. "Hānai", as she called the Queen, raised her from infancy, gave her her own name, Lydia, educated her and made her a member of the royal household for almost 40 years. "I wish I knew why the Queen sent for me," Miss ʻAholo said. "I have never known why." Photo courtesy of Kamehameha Schools/ Bernice Pauahi Bishop Estate Archives

Royal Order of Kamehameha.

ABOVE:

Kamehameha Statue decorated for Kamehameha Day celebrations.

ABOVE:
'Iolani Palace lights.
RIGHT:
Palace draped in black. "First Night" torch light ceremony in observance of the 100th year of the overthrow of the Hawaiian Monarchy.

Directly after the overthrow, January 17, 1893, members of the Royal Hawaiian Band went on strike in protest. They asked composer Ellen Prendergast to compose them a song of rebellion expressing their loyalty to Lili'uokalani. They refused to sign the new government's pledge of support saying, "Rather, we will be satisfied with all that is left to us, the stones, the mystic food of our native land". Prendergast wrote this song, originally called "Mele 'Ai Pōhaku" (Stone-eating Song). It was considered sacred and later, it became known as "Kaulana nā Pua" (Famous Are the Children).

Kaulana Nā Pua

Famous are the children of Hawai'i
Ever loyal to the land
When the evil-hearted messenger comes
With his greedy document of extortion.

Hawai'i, land of Keawe answers.
Pi'ilani's bays help.
Mano's Kaua'i lends support
And so do the sands of Kakuhihewa.

No one will fix a signature
To the paper of the enemy
With its sin of annexation
And sale of native rights.

We do not value
The government's sum of money.
We are satisfied with the stones,
Astonishing food of the land.

We back Lili'u-lani
Who has won the rights of the land.
(She will be crowned again)
Tell the story
Of the people who love their land.

Ellen Wright Prendergast
January 1893

January 17, 1993

ABOVE:

Lili'uokalani's statue decorated for the Centennial of the overthrow of the Hawaiian monarchy.

RIGHT:

From top left; Princess Ka'iulani, King Kalākaua, Kamehameha I, Ka'ahumanu, King Lunalilo, Prince Albert, Queen Emma, Queen Lili'uokalani.

“E
‘onipa‘a
i ka ‘imi
na‘auao”

Be
steadfast
in your
search
for
wisdom

Lili‘uokalani’s
motto

Kamehameha I

1759 (approx.) - 1819
United the Hawaiian Kingdom in 1810

Kamehameha II

Liholiho
Birth: 1797 (approx.)
Accession: 1819
Death: 1824

Kamehameha III

Kauikeaouli
Birth: 1813
Accession: 1824
Death: 1854

Kamehameha IV

Alexander Liholiho
Birth: 1834
Accession: 1854
Death: 1863

Kamehameha V

Lot Kapuāiwa
Birth: 1830
Accession: 1863
Death:1872

King Lunalilo

William Charles Lunalilo
Birth: 1835
Elected: 1873
Death: 1874

King Kalākaua

David Kalākaua
Birth: 1836
Elected: 1874
Death: 1891

Queen Lili'uokalani

Lydia Lili'uokalani Dominis
Birth: 1838
Succeeded: 1891
Deposed: 1893
Death: 1917

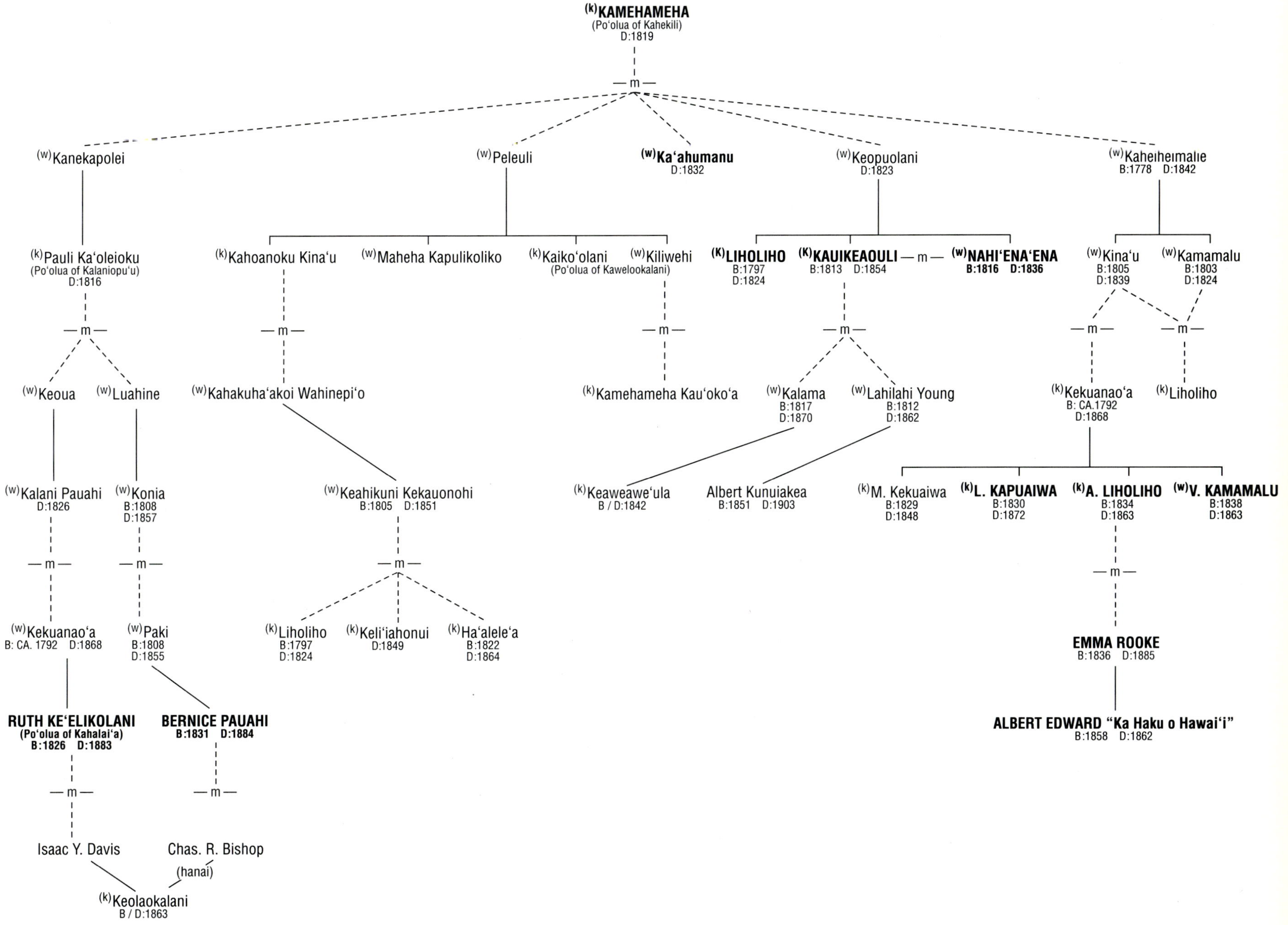

(k)KAMEHAMEHA
(Po'olua of Kahekili)
D:1819

— m —

(w)Kanekapolei
- (k)Pauli Ka'oleioku (Po'olua of Kalaniopu'u) D:1816
  — m —
  - (w)Keoua
    - (w)Kalani Pauahi D:1826
      — m —
      - (w)Kekuanao'a B: CA. 1792 D:1868
        - **RUTH KE'ELIKOLANI (Po'olua of Kahalai'a) B:1826 D:1883**
          — m —
          - Isaac Y. Davis
  - (w)Luahine
    - (w)Konia B:1808 D:1857
      — m —
      - (w)Paki B:1808 D:1855
        - **BERNICE PAUAHI B:1831 D:1884**
          — m —
          - Chas. R. Bishop

Isaac Y. Davis, Chas. R. Bishop (hanai) — (k)Keolaokalani B / D:1863

(w)Peleuli
- (k)Kahoanoku Kina'u
  — m —
  - (w)Kahakuha'akoi Wahinepi'o
    - (w)Keahikuni Kekauonohi B:1805 D:1851
      — m —
      - (k)Liholiho B:1797 D:1824
      - (k)Keli'iahonui D:1849
      - (k)Ha'alele'a B:1822 D:1864
- (w)Maheha Kapulikoliko
- (k)Kaiko'olani (Po'olua of Kawelookalani)
- (w)Kiliwehi
  — m —
  - (k)Kamehameha Kau'oko'a

(w)Ka'ahumanu D:1832

(w)Keopuolani D:1823
- **(K)LIHOLIHO** B:1797 D:1824
- **(K)KAUIKEAOULI** B:1813 D:1854 — m — **(w)NAHI'ENA'ENA B:1816 D:1836**
  — m —
  - (w)Kalama B:1817 D:1870
    - (k)Keaweawe'ula B / D:1842
  - (w)Lahilahi Young B:1812 D:1862
    - Albert Kunuiakea B:1851 D:1903

(w)Kaheiheimalie B:1778 D:1842
- (w)Kina'u B:1805 D:1839
- (w)Kamamalu B:1803 D:1824
  — m —
  - (k)Kekuanao'a B: CA.1792 D:1868
    - (k)M. Kekuaiwa B:1829 D:1848
    - **(k)L. KAPUAIWA** B:1830 D:1872
    - **(k)A. LIHOLIHO** B:1834 D:1863
      — m —
      - **EMMA ROOKE** B:1836 D:1885
        - **ALBERT EDWARD "Ka Haku o Hawai'i"** B:1858 D:1862
    - **(w)V. KAMAMALU** B:1838 D:1863
  — m —
  - (k)Liholiho

K (Kane) = Male
W (Wahine) = Female

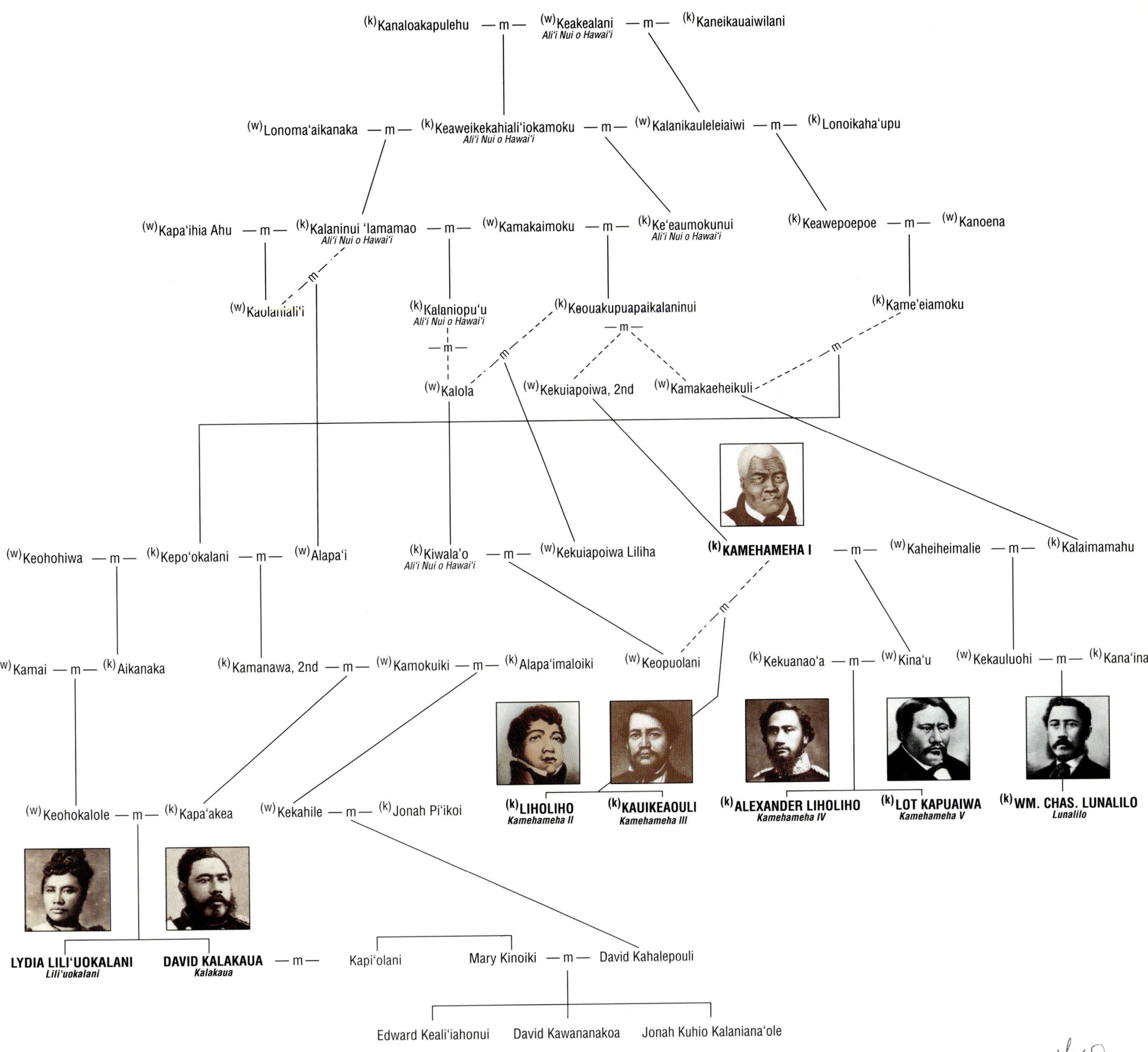

(k) Kanaloakapulehu — m — (w) Keakealani — m — (k) Kaneikauaiwilani
Ali'i Nui o Hawai'i
(w) Lonoma'aikanaka — m — (k) Keaweikekahiali'iokamoku — m — (w) Kalanikauleleiaiwi — m — (k) Lonoikaha'upu
Ali'i Nui o Hawai'i
(w) Kapa'ihia Ahu — m — (k) Kalaninui 'Iamamao — m — (w) Kamakaimoku — m — (k) Ke'eaumokunui
Ali'i Nui o Hawai'i
Ali'i Nui o Hawai'i
(k) Keawepoepoe — m — (w) Kanoena
(w) Kaolaniali'i
(k) Kalaniopu'u
Ali'i Nui o Hawai'i
(k) Keouakupuapaikalaninui
(k) Kame'eiamoku
(w) Kalola
(w) Kekuiapoiwa, 2nd
(w) Kamakaeheikuli
(w) Keohohiwa — m — (k) Kepo'okalani — m — (w) Alapa'i
(k) Kiwala'o — m — (w) Kekuiapoiwa Liliha
Ali'i Nui o Hawai'i
(k) KAMEHAMEHA I — m — (w) Kaheiheimalie — m — (k) Kalaimamahu
(w) Kamai — m — (k) Aikanaka
(k) Kamanawa, 2nd — m — (w) Kamokuiki — m — (k) Alapa'imaloiki
(w) Keopuolani
(k) Kekuanao'a — m — (w) Kina'u
(w) Kekauluohi — m — (k) Kana'ina
(k) LIHOLIHO
Kamehameha II
(k) KAUIKEAOULI
Kamehameha III
(k) ALEXANDER LIHOLIHO
Kamehameha IV
(k) LOT KAPUAIWA
Kamehameha V
(k) WM. CHAS. LUNALILO
Lunalilo
(w) Keohokalole — m — (k) Kapa'akea
(w) Kekahile — m — (k) Jonah Pi'ikoi
LYDIA LILI'UOKALANI
Lili'uokalani
DAVID KALAKAUA
Kalakaua
— m — Kapi'olani
Mary Kinoiki — m — David Kahalepouli
Edward Keali'iahonui
David Kawananakoa
Jonah Kuhio Kalaniana'ole
©
K (Kane) = Male
W (Wahine) = Female

PHOTO NOTES

Page 10 Queen Kapiʻolani, Hawaiʻi State Archives. Stamps and covers, Don Medcalf Collection.

Page 11 Monarchy stamps, bottom right: Liliʻuokalani portrait: Digital compositing by Holly Joy Lau.

Pages 22, 23 ʻIe ʻie baskets, bottom right: fish trap. Faithfully reproduced in the ancient way by Patrick Horimoto.

Page 33 Queen Kamāmalu portrait courtesy Kamehameha Schools/ Bernice Pauahi Bishop Estate.

Page 34, 35 Photos courtesy of Hawaiʻi State Archives.

Page 40 Photo props, antique desk accessories, courtesy David Cornwell Collection.

Page 42 Stationery with Queen Emma residence pictured, Don Medcalf Collection.

Page 50, 51 Charles Bishop's desk, Bernice Pauahi Bishop books and cup and saucer, courtesy Kamehameha Schools/ Bernice Pauahi Bishop Estate.

Pages 62, 63 Hand-colored polaroid transfers of Kalākaua and ʻIolani Palace by the author.

Page 68, 69 Entry way to ʻĀinahau photo courtesy of David Cornwell Collection. Likelike letter Don Medcalf Collection.

Page 75 Period guns, cartridges and Hawaiian flag, courtesy David Cornwell Collection.

Back Cover (Bottom right) Envelope that carried the documents which recognized the Provisional Government of the Hawaiian Island, January 17, 1893, courtesy of Don Medcalf Collection.